T0065549

LESSONS AND LECTURES TO LIVE BY

COLLECTION ONE

Doctor M. E. Lyons

authorHOUSE®

AuthorHouse™
1663 Liberty Drive
Bloomington, IN 47403
www.authorhouse.com
Phone: 1 (800) 839-8640

Published by AuthorHouse 08/25/2016

ISBN: 978-1-5246-2620-4 (sc)
ISBN: 978-1-5246-2619-8 (e)

Print information available on the last page.

Any people depicted in stock imagery provided by Thinkstock are models,
and such images are being used for illustrative purposes only.
Certain stock imagery © Thinkstock.

This book is printed on acid-free paper.

Because of the dynamic nature of the Internet, any web addresses or links contained in
this book may have changed since publication and may no longer be valid. The views
expressed in this work are solely those of the author and do not necessarily reflect the
views of the publisher, and the publisher hereby disclaims any responsibility for them.

KJV
Scripture quotations marked KJV are from the Holy Bible, King James Version
(Authorized Version). First published in 1611. Quoted from the KJV Classic
Reference Bible, Copyright © 1983 by The Zondervan Corporation.

A Word of Thanks

It is through teaching and lecturing that we have the prized privilege to dig deep in the Word of God and share it with those who are eager to hear what God has to say. Upon reading this book one will see quickly that these lessons and lectures will speak life and guidance into your life.

About This Book

This book is packed with spiritually driven lessons to live by. Lessons that will inspire, touch and enable you to peek into the depths of the scriptures. Upon reading this book one will experience the riches of the Word from a lesson's perspective.

Contents

Lesson One

"I've Fallen And I Can't Get Up"
Luke 18:1

Actually this prayer or para-blay does not teach us to pray...

It teaches us HOW to pray...
Fervor and frequency of prayer
Constancy and perseverance

To omit prayer is to assume battle without a battalion...
It's like working in the sun without a morning meal...
It's like boarding a plane without a pilot...
It's like driving a vehicle without a steering wheel...

You are moving but without knowledge of where you are going...
You are destined to dismount at a destination that has no design...

Real prayer is hard...
Real prayer consists of fainting work...

I might lose you right through here...but real prayer is harder than preaching!

If you don't believe me: God is all powerful...preaching is God speaking to and through us...

But praying is us talking to God!
You still missed it...preaching is using His strength...praying is using our strength...

We do not believe what we profess and what we pray…
We do not feel what we pray
We do not wish what we petition
Because if we ask…we do not go about it correctly…

If we did…we would pray in the house
By the way
Places of businesses
In our beds
On the highways
Everywhere

We would pray constantly…but what we do is we pray and then worry…

One writer says if we pray or a harvest we ought to get up off our knees with a basket to reap in our hands…

Watch this: if water continuously drops; it will eventually wear a hole in the hardest of stones…

Dr. Luke the Physician uses a familiar medical metaphor to share with us about this prayer concept…

He says: pray and not faint…he hints at the idea that prayer is tedious…
We use to say tarry in prayer…
This particular parable has the key hanging on the door, but many times we attempt to break the door down when we possess the key!

Instead of praying and then waiting…pray and keep on praying…because waiting without praying suggests that you do not need to communicate to the one who can comment and contribute your circumstance…

When he uses the strong word ought it suggest on one hand and subpoenas on another…

Suggestion is it is a privilege…because there is something in prayer that is beneficial…but the in the subpoena it states that it's something that must be done or you will pay the penalty of being without his assistance…

Ought is a derivative of thought and what this story teaches us that our thoughts arrest our thoughts from time to time.

Usually when we do not pray it is because your thoughts have caused your heart to faint…

You see when we fall into troublesome times it will either cause us to faint or pray…either we will have days of fear or days of faith…

During World War II, when the bombing was so massive and intense in London a sign was placed in front of a local Church that read:
"If your knees knock, kneel."

This must happen by dint of importunity…
(Otherwise by working at persevering…)

As we study this scripture on Eastern culture and setting; the courtroom is not the courtroom we know today…but was a tent that was moved from place to place as the judge covered and traveled the entire circuit…

The judge, not the law set the agenda and as he sat in the tent surrounded by his assistants, anybody could watch the proceedings from the outside of the tent…but only those who were approved and accepted could have their cases tried…
This usually took place through bribing the assistants so that the judge would call their case…

Watch this: the obstacles this woman endured…
1. She was a woman…women did not go to court
2. She was a widow…so she had no husband to go for her
3. She was poor so she could not pay or bribe even if she desired… all she had was prayer…

Doctor M. E. Lyons

If we do not pray…we will faint-lose heart-
Give up
Quit
Succumb

Fainting-you feel yourself slipping and you cannot do anything about it…

Listen; there is a connection between Luke 18:1 and Luke 17:37 in English Standard Version:
And they said to him, "Where, Lord?" He said to them, "Where the corpse is, there the vultures will gather."

If our surroundings are likened unto a rotting corpse, then the atmosphere we live in has become inundated with pollutants…and will ultimately have an effect on our spiritual lives…

BUT…when we pray we inhale the pure air of Heaven…keeps us from fainting…

Not constantly repeating the same prayer…Always does not suggest this…

But rather to make prayer acquiesce to being as our regular breathing has become…

You see because unless we are sick, asphyxiated or suffocated we never think about breathing…we just do it…it is happenstance by automaticity!

Prayer should be natural for a believer
It should be a habit…folk should expect prayer from you
(Counseling, Meetings, anytime we come together at the Church for anything…they say we know you are going to pray…)

Prayer should be the atmosphere in which we live…
Prayer is more than linguistic levels; it should be our lifestyle…

Question in closing:
Would we rather pray (the way the scripture outlines…) or faint?

Lesson Two

"An Attitude Adjustment"
Philippians 2:5

Mind here means attitude.

This text is about humility in the mind; attitude.

We always said your attitude determines your altitude.

The attitude of Christ was to be about His father's business.

He thought of others not Himself.

If satan can give us a jacked up attitude he has won, the battle.

Because what he fears the most; he attacks the most; come on think about satan gets most of us by getting us to DEVELOP an attitude concerning our gifts

Watch this: our gifts are only a deposit that others might withdraw from

We need to realize we are only managers of that which has been deposited in us; so when we have the attitude of I have arrived

Or should I say:
Can't nobody preach like me
Sing like me
Pray like me
Speak like me

When this happens we relieve humility to allow pride to recline

That's why He says earlier look not on the things of yourself but rather on the things of others; because your fruit is not for you; it's for somebody else!

You see his attacks: mark our assignment

Many times we are dismissed from our assignments because our attitudes have sent word to our appointments to cancel our arrival

When Jesus went back home to Nazareth; they attacked Him

The question that is being asked in the text that we are to consider tonight; asks why did Jesus go back.

Because, He wanted to help folk from the place He came from

He made special trips there to assist His acquaintances

Get this: His guilt arises out of knowing where He came from; and then leading folk out of what He left them in

It was not in the geographical place He was from, it was psychologically economically, and spiritually where He was from.

Our problem is that when God brings us from a place, we tend to disremember the dilemma we were in

Be it promiscuity
Lying
Backbiting
Idolatry
Wandering eyes and following acts

We were there; I am still in the text.

He went back to His hometown because this scripture says He took on the form of a servant and in the likeness of men

The word likeness- hah-moy-a-mah; which means a copy.

What keeps us from possessing this mind is; we desire suppressing what we should be expressing and ends up being repression!
(Hiding unpleasant experiences)

Otherwise we tuck away our testimonies
Hide our helps
Cover up our challenges
Mismanage our maladies
Misrepresent our mess-ups

Attempting to have our mind and attitudes supersede His

And if you have not been drug through hell there is no way you can tell me what potholes to watch out for and how much dirt to expect

But when you are ready to share with me that you have been where I am going you display the mind of Christ

I wish I had time: ego (the I of a person, the part of us which reacts to the world), superego (conscience, personality), and the id (unconscious, instinctive)

Help others who struggle with what we are struggling with ourselves

This scripture proves to me that God works on the theatre of my thoughts which is my attitude

God can hear our mind which is our attitude.

That is why He says; Let THIS Mind, because creators hear the imperfections and impediments in their creations
(Mechanics; just crank it up)

This mind is where decisions bully our destinations and ultimately our destiny.

His mind seeks questions; whereas our mind seek answers

What is the mind of Christ?
To wash feet

W.W.J.D. is what Philippians 2:5 is saying to us...
Hate that brother
Talk about that sister
Lie
Run rumors

Let- means think; if I think about food then my mind envisions food.

Because something must associate the mind with the matter

He was humble; don't miss this.

He says I was powerful; still humble

Able
Capable
Apt
Gifted

He was consumed in humility

There is so much responsibility entrusted to the word humility that it is one of the major components of a better world: II Chronicles 7:14
You cannot pray for humility He says you need to be humble before you pray. Because you know too much!

The Holy Writ says: let this mind; someone may say we are supposed to have the mind of Christ; NO

Our finite, fickled and fallible frames could not contain the mind of Christ

But we could possess the attitude of Christ; that's why He had to lower himself

Our attitudes are what others see; and our mind is simply the projector!

If you don't believe me; let somebody have a bad/ stinky, and messed up attitude nothing is considered or heard concerning their thoughts because their attitude is nasty

Catch this: when He says: this

It is as if there is a proverbial finger that arises from this text and points back to the text and say THIS MIND

Because this particular passage was spoken demonstratively and in 3rd person in a divine passive voice which is of God

Otherwise, God says Paul is not just speaking, he is repeating what I told him to say

In other words, what you perfect is that, but what He perfects is THIS In- means it becomes you and there is no more coaching it becomes culture!

Our attitude is really a direct reflection of what we believe our needs are

Lesson Three

"Are We Getting The Job Done?"
Matthew 9:35-38

Are we concerned about the right thing?
When people are more concerned about who comes to visit them and who does not come to visit them...rather than the lost being saved...

Are we concerned about the right thing?
When folk will have a holy conniption over who counts the money and who doesn't, rather than a wayward soul to be reclaimed...

Are we concerned about the right thing?
When Pastor/Preachers are driven on how many folks are in the congregation than how many are not on the outside...

Are we concerned about the right thing?
When auxiliaries are so focused on Annual days that Annual deaths without Christ are taking place...

Are we concerned about the right thing?
When we as a people of God spend more time in these four walls than we do witnessing in the highways and byways...

People are looking for a way out.
Searching for an answer to their problems.
Wishing their storms would cease.
Hoping for a better day.
Studying to find a better way.

Using their money to try and find happiness, whilst we shut ourselves up in the confines of these four walls.

We sing our hymns, pray our prayers, and preach our messages to a people that know the way; while others who are lost continue to waste away. Church folk have become so comfortable, agreeable, relaxed, undisturbed, untroubled, and at ease with meeting in these suitable accommodations that we fail to realize the hurt on the outside.

It's sad to know that there are others of the human species that struggle and strain while we rest and relax.

We have made our responsibility shift from going to wherever the lost is, and we now wait for the lost to come to us.

Jesus looked at the crowds following him and referred to them as a field ripe for harvest.

Notice the reason he wanted them to go into the field was he was moved with compassion.

Some of us need to be moved with compassion even now.

Look on the news;
Babies having babies
Men having families everywhere.
Teenagers shooting up schools.

Jesus was moved with compassion based off what he saw in the crowd and their need and void that needed to be met.

Same sex marriages
Prayer in school
Educational laziness
Marital martyrs
Field ripe for the harvest.

We spend too much time in here and no time out there.
(Jehovah Witnesses- when was the last time someone who was a Christian knocked on your door.)
You see you don't pick what is already picked.

Otherwise we cannot expect for God to be excited about us meeting up here every week and shouting and going home.

We can't save those who are already saved.

Many people are ready to give their lives to Christ if would someone would tell them how.

Let's see Paul said it like this in; Galatians 6:9

And let us not be weary in well doing: for in due season we shall reap, if we faint not.

Now watch this Paul simply says when we act out what we were created for, we shall reap

Two things he says don't get tired of actually doing; action word.

Don't get tired of doing what you are told to do for in due season; otherwise he'll pay you when it's time.

It is something you owe.

You missed it if you plant and work now when it comes to pass your reward will come to pass.

Now let me share this with you, Jesus said; the harvest truly is plenteous, but the laborers are few.

Watch this: Jesus is out teaching and preaching and stops in the middle of it all, the hustle and bustle and notices so much going on; and instead

of preaching to the ones who the disciples thought needed it He switched audiences
(He is talking to them)

Many times we think it's for everybody else when it really is for us!!!

Jesus called Peter to the carpet one day about how he may have thought he had arrived; Luke 22:32

Now catch this: many of us have been convicted but not converted. (Conviction will cause us to cry and say Lord I am sorry; but conversion means I am turning directions so that I might help somebody else. Peter I know you have been baptized but when you really are tired of doing what you are doing and become converted; THEN strengthen the brethren!)

Pray that the Lord of the harvest will send some workers.

The abnormal or eccentric perception of this idea is that Jesus really implies here that everyone has their season to be a reaper.

He says the harvest is ready to be reaped.

I used to think that there was no such thing as you being in your season but this open my eyes to this ideology.

He says we only have a little while to reap those who are ready to be harvested or picked.

You do know what happens whenever you don't pick or gather what is ripe don't you?

It rots.
It will shrivel up.
It will die.

No different here; He says when we do not try and reach the ones who are ready; then we miss the opportunity to save the lost.

Jesus says pray that we receive more workers.

He needs workers that know how to deal with folk problems.

Jesus commands for us to pray that people would respond to the need for laborers.

When we pray for something many times God uses us as a part of the remedy.
(Lord help them; He turns and uses you to help them)

Verse 38 says "Pray he would send laborers <u>into</u> the harvest."

(I know we don't want to hear this but if we don't go into these crack houses, prostitutes' places, gang infested neighborhoods, violent streets and witness it will not be done.)

He said into

We cannot harvest away from the harvest.

It's like picking grapes in the supermarket; you didn't pick them you are just picking them up, but somebody else actually picked the grapes.

When Jesus said send forth- it carries with it the meaning of thrust forth.

In this context it means to give someone a strong push into the field.
Can I say it like the scripture says it?

We need a little pep talk, a strong urging, a reminder what we are really here to do.

Field is a term most folk use on a job.

Story:
Martin Luther had a friend who believed just as he did in the faith.

What this friend would do was to pray for Martin Luther as he went down into the villages and areas to witness, and one day this friend fell asleep and had a dream that Martin Luther was in the middle of this field the size of the world and when he was able to see anybody he saw one man and he made the face out and noticed it was Martin Luther; he then saw the real truth and said "I must leave my prayers and get to work."

Some of us need to leave our prayers and go to work.

Watch this he calls them to pray right here; but in the very next chapter they are sent out.

Enter to worship depart to serve.

Lesson Four

"Do You Know What Today Is?"
Psalms 118:24

Introduction: Have you in your marriage been walking around and out of nowhere your wife or husband says: "Do you know what today is" the reason they ask is because you are not acting like you remember…child's birthday…special day…

There is a reason he says…THIS…because our focus should only be on right now…not down the road…that is what messes up our days… worrying about our nights…

This scripture speaks to Christ's resurrection and he is literally saying you ought to be glad because he died and rose and THIS DAY would not be possible if He had not died…

1 Thessalonians 5:16 Rejoice evermore.

Often we forget what today is --- today is a day made by our God for us … God's design for this day is very clear and concise --- CELEBRATE… ENJOY LIFE…Today has a DIVINE PURPOSE…

Psalm 118:24- This is the day which the Lord hath made;
(You see the word made has housed within it…that anything that is made has components or ingredients…)

We will rejoice and be glad in it.

Psalm 118:24- This is the very day God acted on in our behalf

— Let's celebrate and be festive!

This is the day God gave us
This is the day God blessed us with
This is the day God has allowed
This is the day that God has gifted us with…so what can we do with it…
it's simple…
Let's rejoice…

Now can we deal with the word RE-JOICE…?
To have joy all over again…
To joy again…

Often New Testament believers greeted one another with the word:
REJOICE!

-We now greet one another with sadness
Sickness
Sorrow
Mess
Discouragement
Gossip

But what's wrong with reverting back to the way they used to do it in the Biblical days…

Wouldn't it be encouraging…to perhaps have had a pretty rough day… and one of our Christians brothers walk up and say…THIS IS THE DAY THAT THE LORD HATH MADE; LET US REJOICE AND BE GLAD IN IT…

So rejoice was a salutation expressing a good wish for a blessing upon a person!

There was a reason why the Bible says: LET US…because we ought to have true koinonia…FELLOWSHIP with one another…no one ought to have to go through anything in the physical by themselves…LET US…

Watch this:
GOD MADE TODAY! GOD MADE TODAY FOR US! GOD MADE TODAY FOR US TO REJOICE AND BE GLAD...

Not to weep as with no hope
Not to drag
Not to give up
Not to hang our heads down...but to rejoice...

Philippians 3:1 Finally, my brethren, rejoice in the Lord..... otherwise after everything is said and done...REJOICE...

One literary tool is the power of repetition...

C. Paul knew the literary tool of repetition:

Philip. 4:4 Rejoice in the Lord always: and again I say, Rejoice.
The only way to do this is IN THE LORD...

Joy is the fruit of a right relationship with god...

Joy is not something people can create by fleshly methods...
A state of well-being that comes from knowing and serving God.

JOY is found over 150 times in the Bible.
Include joyful, joyous --- it tops 200 times.
The word REJOICE is in the Bible over 200 times.

<u>God like joy is found in some strange places...</u>

Barren Sarah declares: GOD HAS MADE ME LAUGH... Gen. 21:6
Barren Hannah finds JOY in her dysfunctional home, even before God answers her prayer. Hannah rejoiced before Samuel's birth.
1 Samuel 2:1
The people of God were working in the VALLEY, they REJOICED when they saw the ark of the covenant was coming home...

1 Samuel 6:13
God's joy can make us rejoice when things don't appear to be good... God joy will lead singing when in jail...

James 1:2 My brethren, count it all joy when ye fall into divers temptations;

Know when to rejoice... This day is created for rejoicing...

We will waste this day if we do not find the heart of rejoicing...

We must recognize what today is...

    A. If you can't be happy where you are --- What makes you think you will be happy in another place?

    B. Joy is made --- not found.

Romans 12:15 Rejoice with them that do rejoice, and weep
With them that weep.
(We don't practice this enough...if we did; we would be saying to those who are down...REJOICE...instead of talking about them or looking down on them...)

How can we have joy...?

    1. JOY --- J-esus first, O-thers second, Y-ourself last...
    2. Be CONTENT where ever you find yourself!
    3. Speak smooth words, they are easier to eat...
    4. Never focus on anything but what is true, honest, just, pure, lovely, virtue and good report.

(These were words of encouragement to the believers...Phil. 4:8)

CONCLUSION:

Do you know what today is?
Make up your mind to rejoice and be glad in it...

He says in it...because we don't know what the next moment may bring!

Lesson Five

"Dressed For Success"
Ephesians 6: 10-18

Intro: On a job interview, when you meet someone for the very first time, or in the presence of an admired person; you put on your best to impress.

We are supposed to not only look our best to impress the one who's presence we are in, but we are to procure or prepare ourselves for what we are about to enter.

If you were going to a pool party I dare not put on a suit
If you were going to a social gathering, I will not show up in shorts and a t-shirt
If you were coming to church would you come with pajamas on?
If you were going to a banquet would you show up with bath robe on?

No you would come dressed for the occasion.

Listen, this is what Paul is sharing with us; you ought to be dressed for the occasion.

Not only should you be dressed for the occasion, but you should be dressed ready for success.

You cannot expect to swim fast with a Sunday go to meeting outfit on, you need something suitable for that occasion.

Paul has just finished speaking to the church at Ephesus (us) about our home lives.

Children, obey your parents in the Lord: for this is right.
(Starts at the bottom and works his way up)
HONOUR THY FATHER AND MOTHER; (which is the first
commandment with a promise;)
(Notice the strange capitalizations in this passage of scripture)

Whenever I am typing and I want to convey a message and let you hear in
what voice I am thinking I use capital letters, all Paul was sharing with us
in the scripture and the next is that Honor is essential or important when
dealing with your parents because if you do not Honor (high respect) your
parent(s) notice the s on the end he says God promised it first and secondly
however long you were supposed to live has been cut short.

Then Paul moves to the Fathers and says don't instigate, irritate, anger,
rouse up; I know we don't like this part but don't do things that you know
that will upset them; the scripture says this.
(Now watch this; the message that Paul is trying to send or convey is that
in order for you to become prepared for what is to come you have to have
your house in order.)

If you don't have your house in order there is no way you can win.

A house divided cannot stand; I know you probably where I am going
with this.

We cannot come to church or any other place trying to lead there if we are
ineffective in our own house.
(In the book Wisdom of the Ages one writer says in there if you ever have
to go around telling people you are the leader then chances are you are not)

Then Paul says to the public arena servants, workers, whomever you have
that is the source of your income; be obedient to them, then he says do it
as if you were doing it for Christ.
(You see many times we can become so angry, disgruntled, dissatisfied
with our employers that we do not remember nor see that the scripture says
obey them as if Jesus was your Supervisor, Manager, Foreman)

The question is would you do to Jesus what you do to your boss; would you say to Jesus what you say to your Boss

Do you skip out on Jesus as you do your Boss; early, take long breaks, etc.

O.k. then watch this Paul says Christ wants you to not do what you do on your jobs for the sake of a bonus

That's too heavy
Not for a bonus
Not for a pat on the back
Not for a stipend
Not for self-gain
Not for appreciation
Not to please them

But whatever you do even in the secular perform your abilities' and responsibilities as servants of Chris; oh but watch this not only as servants of Christ but also to fulfill the will of God.

You mean to tell me when I go to work whatever I do there is supposedly to fill the will of God; yes, but that is not all.

He then places an indicator on that; he says let it be the will of God not just outwardly but inwardly.

Watch this man looks at the outward but God looks at the heart, so he says the only way God recognizes your performance in whatever you do outside is by his will being carried out and he honors it by the intent of your heart. So if you are on the job, working in church, wherever you maybe you may look like you are doing the right thing, but if your heart is not matching with your work it will not only affect what is about to come, but it will come as disobedience to your father.

I really don't want you to miss this when he opens and says Children obey... he not only is speaking to 0-18-year old's he is speaking to his children, because remember he claims us as his children.

Paul closes this portion and says that whatever you do right

- – treating others right when they have done you wrong
- – helping those in need
- – doing what is expected of you

Whatever thing you do right, you will receive requital for it from the Lord. (The Lord will reward you)

Now that's alright but now that Paul has laid that groundwork he now shifts gears and says finally, my brethren be strong in the Lord; otherwise when you get this together there more to come.

He shares with us that we need to armor up
We need to get dressed for success

Otherwise you can have success unless you are dressed with what is to be explained.

Listen as he says put on the whole armor of God, that ye may be able to stand the wiles of the devil.

It's like this you cannot overcome with anything other than the armor of God, now don't become too anxious to believe that you can possess some of these pieces of armor and still win; it is impossible to win half-covered.

Paul opens this classic scripture saying we don't wrestle against flesh and blood.

Now let me explain something here we spend so much time fighting amongst ourselves about things we have no business doing!

This help me not to long ago about Negro's who are determined to do things their way, and no their way.

Watch this, when someone talks about you
When someone rumors on you

When someone agitates you
When someone
When someone does wrong to you

Realize it's not really them, it's a Spirit.
(Daddy would say something to me and others when he was explaining why he distanced himself at times when folk would do him wrong or tell a lie)

He would say I don't dislike them, I just dislike their ways; watch this God says I am holy and I cannot stand to look at ungodliness.

Don't lose me now, whatever you do to me is not necessarily what you are doing or saying it is the Spirit you have allowed to control you at that moment.

You see we have the power to allow sprits to control us.

So when you do wrong to me
Lie on me
Ridicule
Talk behind my back your back

It's not them it's a Spirit they have given power to.

You don't believe me it's in the text.

Verse 12

For we wrestle not against flesh and blood- that's us, but against principalities, against powers, against the rulers of the darkness of this world, against Spiritual wickedness in high places.

That's why I love the scripture Romans 8:38-39

Watch how he places the next scripture in a perfectly synchronized order.
(He repeats himself by implying to gear up)

take unto yourself the whole armor of God, but beloved listen how he concludes that 13th verse he says having done all; what do you mean all.

I'll tell you what he meant when he said all, all that I have shared with you concerning your:

- Children
- Fathers
- Jobs, etc.
- Church
- Fulfilling his will
- Preparing yourselves

Otherwise after you've done all of that and dressed for success, STAND

Now that's weird why would we do all that work and get dressed to just stand there?

I mean he just leaves us standing there, he tells us what to put on but nothing to do but stand.

There was a reporter that interviewed a man on his 100th birthday! He asked "what are you most proud of?" the man said, "I don't have an enemy in the world." Wouldn't that be a beautiful thing! The reporter said, "How did you accomplish this feat" the man said, "To be honest, I outlived every last one of my enemies."

I guess what I am saying is when you let God fight for you; you can outlast your enemies.

The armor of God is not something you put on everyday like a pair of jeans or a dress

The belt of truth

In these days' Roman soldiers wore thick, wide leather belts that held their swords and other equipment.

Whenever they girded up their belt they were ready to fight; it was what held everything together.

The truth which is translated aletheia is and should be an essential centerpiece of a Christian's life.

It should be on the truth that everything we believe in rests.

Understand satan is a liar, and whenever we try to live by the truth he comes to place a lie in our life that we might not be fully prepared to handle his attack.

Without truth we have no morals about ourselves
- shacking it's a lie band it is immoral
- stealing- it's a lie because it is not because you are practicing what should be but is not; and it is immoral

We now have married people acting like single people and single people acting like married couples. It's a lie.

Lying in itself is immoral because it is simply not the truth.
Watch this in the middle, or at the core of truth is integrity; integrity is moral uprightness; honesty, wholeness, soundness.

One of the things that I thank God I inherited of my father was that of not being able to stand a liar.
- Watch this my innate lie detector tells me this
- If a man or woman cannot look at me while talking to me in my eye, I question their truthfulness and their integrity.

(We used to hear from parents if you lied and looked them in the face we would say you are a ball-faced lie.)
- You will have a clear conscience when you stand on the truth.
- You can stand on the truth and sleep at night when others wrestle at night because you are dressed for success when they are up fighting the Spirits they have invited in and gave room to.
- Gird yourself; otherwise secure yourself.
- Gird- Girdle it holds back everything that you don't want to let out.

37

(Up at the high school one of the things that bothers me so much about the young men is that they walk around sagging, with their pants hanging off; one arm swinging the other arm holding up their pants and their legs spread eagle trying to walk)

You know when you don't have a belt on your pants fall and you are subject to slip, fall, and expose yourself, among other things.

It's the same way Spiritually whenever you leave the belt of truth off, you struggle trying to even make it because everything that you are trying to cover up is exposed.

You not only expose yourself but you cripple yourself- no place for you to get a good stance
You cannot secure your equipment
Your hands are not free to hold the shield and the sword.

Well not only should truth be a part of you and your everyday life.

But truth is immutable.

- You see a lie you have to speak a lie, but truth will just happen.
- Think about it in order for something to be a lie somebody has said something that was not true.
- Let me say it like this a lie can live; but only for a while.
- But truth will live forever.
- Folk can cover lies and they hold for a moment

Prejudice is dead-in presidential race even now.
A lie can live only so long.

No one has the authority or ability to manipulate the truth.

Have you ever tried to live a lie?

you have a lot of money but don't
you are married and really are not

you have a higher position in the company than you really have
you are more Spiritual than you really are
you are about to have something that you know you aren't; house car- after
so long folk are going to wonder where it is.

It's difficult to live a lie.
Because in order to live a lie you have to keep up a façade.

But when you live the truth
You be who you are
You say what you say
You act as you act
You just live your life

It is upon the truth of the Gospel of Jesus Christ that we build our lives.
John 8:32

Free from what
Sin- well what does sin breed

- Heartache
- Pain
- Suffering
- Problems
- Obstacles
- Everything your mind could fathom

Let's evaluate this verse

Jesus says and you shall <u>know- the key word is know</u>
Now let us not run through this verse

When Jesus says know he is speaking of a relationship, not interpretation.

Watch this he simply says ye shall know not in the context of how you
comprehend his word
Understand what the bible is saying

Apprehend his divine dictates

He speaks of know in the context of relationship
Listen, when I say I know my wife I could mean three ways
Intimately- I am aware of what she enjoys
Intellectually- I am aware of her thought patterns, I can't tell you what she
is thinking but I am cognitively close.
Informatively- I am aware of what she likes for me to talk about.

Watch this when he says ye shall know;

He is really saying you are aware of what he enjoys,
What he might want you to be thinking
What he would want you to talk about

And because you are so in to Him, it will make you free.

Because you do know that he is truth.
John 14:6

So it's like this if you get to know him, you will know the truth and he
will make you free.

You do know that the verbiage make means to bring about, or to cause
to come.

- Whatever had you bound has to let you go.
- Songwriter said satan had me bound but Jesus lifted me.

Breastplate of Righteousness

- We have what we call bullet-proof vests which is exactly the same
  as what they used back in these days, only difference is that then
  they used armor; today we use Kevlar.
- Why would Paul be so determined for us to cover our chests?
- When you peel away the skin, muscles and protective ribcage you
  have the heart.

You see when something goes wrong with the heart, the body dies.

whenever you guard the heart you are less vulnerable to the attack of satan.

Have you ever had your heart broken?
Someone close to you die?

It's easy to do wrong because you do not care about anything?

You now have contracted this "I don't care attitude"

Well what is righteousness?

Doing what we know to do that is right when we want to do wrong.
Romans 7:21

So guarding our hearts is imperative or important to our survival.

Proverbs 4:23

<u>Watch this; whoever has your heart controls you!!!!!!!!!</u>

When Solomon says keep- he means it is continual process.
I believe that is why the song-writer says "I woke up this morning with my mind..."

Because whatever you allow- key word allow your heart to desire is where your mind and body will follow.

- He says you have to strive at this thing, and not give up do it with diligence,
- Because out of your heart are the issues of life, if you let satan in that will be what your life is categorized by.

Whatever makes it to your heart; it what will dictate to you what you will do!

- Think about it
- Husband/wife- forgive them time and time again
- Fish- it will be number one on your list
- Horse-back riding
- Soap opera-it will precedence over everything else

Whatever you give your heart to will win.

There is only one thing that protects our hearts from satan; righteousness.

Righteousness is about how one stands with God.
- If you do not stand right with God you do not possess righteousness
- If he is secondary to your primary goals, and aspirations, then you have no righteousness.
- If God cannot occupy your time more than anything else, righteousness is not there.
- That's why Peter said listen if you really want this righteousness the Lord says, I Peter 1: 15-16 be holy in all you do, be holy as I am holy.
- So applying the breastplate of righteousness is to live each day in moment by moment in obedience to the Father.

- Listen, turn to Matthew 7:17

- A tree can only produce whatever seed that was accepted in the soil.

- Let me see if can explain this; our minds are our Spiritual soil, and the word of God is the seed, Spiritually or to oppose that any communications or conversations can also be seeds.

- If I plant an apple seed, I cannot expect oranges.

- But on the other side of that, if the ground has not been cultivated, prepared, tilled and ready to receive the seeds, nothing can sprout up.

It's like this just because I am here at church tonight does not mean that

I receive the word, I would have had to pray for God to open and ready my mind to receive what he has for me to apply to my life.

Then if my mind is open for whatever seed is to be planted I can grow to the potential I was created to be.

But if my mind is closed, Spirit has not been prepped; I cannot and will not receive anything.

I can plant something in your mind, but only God can plant it in your Spirit.

So what am I saying, if righteousness is how I live day by day, and my relationship with God, how can I perceive how to live if I don't know the guidelines by which I am to go by.

I guess if I had to ask a question, I would ask.

– What guards your heart, your selfish desires, or the seed that is being planted on Sunday mornings, Wednesday nights, which you might be able to let your heart give life.

Shoes shod with the preparation of the Gospel

– Shoes keep men and women from slipping
– Makes you ready for battle
– What soldiers need more than anything is their traction?

(In boxing if your stance is not right you can get knocked out, if you are standing just right you can hit harder than you are truly able to hit.)

– It's about surefootedness so that you can stand as Paul says.
(If God be for us…, but when we get nervous what limb do we use most our feet; we pace, we wiggle our toes, click our heels, shake our feet if they are crossed.)

Look how Asaph categorized his encounter with him not being ready as of yet; my foot almost slipped, otherwise because I wasn't concerned about my footing I almost went there…

- In our everyday lives, once we put on our shoes we are ready to go.
- We put on everything else and save our shoes for last, most of the times.

This parallels with Spirituality as well, shoes are important Spiritually too.

- Shoes give us mobility

1. It grants us maneuvering strength
   a. Reference Isaiah 40: 31

1. The peace that we need is encapsulated in waiting on God otherwise possessing that peace that calms you.
2. Let me explain something the reason why many of us don't want to witness, or will not witness is because we are weighted down with our own problems.

   a. I got my own stuff I'm dealing with I don't have time for them.
   b. I'm depressed and you want me to go out there and talk with more depressed folk.
   c. I'm barely making ends meet and you want me to help them.

- So what Isaiah has to say about this armor is that if you can wait on God but in the meanwhile be ready now you can renew your strength; you can run, you can walk and not faint and don't forget he says you shall mount up…
- Shoes gives us mobility
- Shoes gives us stability

1. It allows us to have a firmer grip
2. It gives us a better footing
   a. Reference I Corinthians 15:1

1. It gives us stability only if we have the right shoes on;
2. Somebody says right shoes on.
3. If we stand on the physical, we will only believe what we see; I hope you get this.
4. But if we stand on the Spiritual we receive what we don't see.
   a. Otherwise you may not understand how I am going to do it, fix it, or give it but you know I will.
   b. Notice Paul says in Corinthians whatever I have preached is what you stand on; well what did he preach the word, who is the word, Christ is, so if he is the word and I believe what I heard I am in essence standing on Him, and if I am standing on Him the shoes I have on is direct reflection of what I am standing on.
   – shoes give us stability

   – Shoe gives us capability
1. It enables us to do what we couldn't do initially
2. It gives us an ability to do something we weren't able to do before.
   a. Reference right here in this text Ephesians 6:11

1. You are able to stand against the wiles…
2. Otherwise you could not do it if you weren't in the stance.
3. But Paul would not have told us to dress our feet with shoes if they were not able to help us against the wiles of the devil.

Just think for a little while how important shoes are to us today.
   – We'll say put your shoes on I'm ready to go.
   – You can get a ticket without shoes on.

The Roman soldier's shoes even laced up to their calve muscles.
They slept with their shoes on; in case they had to get up running
   – I think we ought to learn from that to always be ready.
   – For shoes is a symbol of readiness.

Preparation means to be ready; not slothful, but alert.
It means to really prepare oneself;

- Listen if there was someone in the street was stranded; and you were led to help, would you say while they are struggling I will help you if you come to my church?

- that's not the method to follow.

Having your shoes on means a few things.
- To be ready, now if you don't have your Spiritual shoes on and have not yet prepared you cannot effectively help.
- You have to have a peace about you that the other person falls in love with in order that they might open up enough to do what you ask.
- We have to learn that religious talk is not always the way to speak to someone who is in need of help. I know you don't agree.

(A member ran across I was the last person they wanted to see; they were high and drunk and was so embarrassed.)

We have to in a discreet way learn how to tell others how to receive peace. Romans 10:15

Second thing about shoes is you cannot win against the enemy without the shoes on.
- Luke 10:9
- Remember I said you cannot put the devil under your feet, well that's right but you can if you have the right shoes on.
- God has given us the victory

Having your shoes on means that you are ready then and there when God calls us to a ministry moment.

Watch this, we are called to share the Gospel with the shoes of peace; nobody signed the evangelism sheet but one…
- It is a disservice to God.

Shield of Faith

- They stood together expanding a mile or more forming one large shield.

- 2 ½ feet wide and 4 ½ tall
- Designed to protect the entire body.
- They would be on the frontlines

The archers would wrap the tips of their arrows w/ cloth and dip them in a pitch or we would call it tar-like substance then set them on fire.

Upon impact the pitch would spatter and burn anything that was not flame retardant.

But the devil does the very same thing; shooting flaming arrows that have the capability to not only harm us but whoever is around us.

Let me see if I can make this crystal clear.

The enemy works like this:

Your marriage is not the utopia (Perfect place or thing) you hoped for so you feel empty and unfulfilled and begin looking for someone else.

You child does something that you don't agree with so you withdraw your affection.

You are the Spiritual covering for that child

You are alone in a motel room on a trip with a friend or business associate, but flesh arises and now your co-worker seems more attractive than your wife or husband.

You go on lunch break with the opposite sex and having problems and discuss them with your fellow employee; they listen and pay more attention than your own spouse

- Satan uses a friend or fellow church member to say some hurtful remarks, words that cut like a knife.

These are fiery darts of the enemy and if you don't have the shield of faith you cannot ward them off.

It affects others because if you don't have the shield of faith:

Your adultery can splatter all over you children
Your infidelity can affect church members who looked up to you
Your neglect your children can affect that child's education
Your disobedience can cause somebody else to make the same mistake

When it hits it goes everywhere.

That's why we wonder when we start doubting God about so many things it affects people we don't even know.

Ask a mother whose child thought they had no reason to live because they did not have faith in God.

- family messed up
- friends messed up
- Church is hurt

So many are affected by our doubt.

We cannot live the way we want to and hope that God will bail us out when we get into trouble.

It cannot be found in living continually in a perpetual state of sin.

It is placing all of our trust in Him
(Putting all of our weight on the truth which is His word and is Him.)

Faith does not operate in the realm of the possible. Faith begins where man's power ends.

Watch this, faith and obedience goes hand in hand.
You cannot have one without the other.

- Proverbs 3:5, 6
- James 2:20
- God's Word Bible translation says: You fool! Do you have to be shown that faith which does nothing is useless?

You can say all day to you pass out I believe but belief breeds action!

- Abraham and his son Isaac
- Rahab the prostitute hid the spies whom Joshua sent over to spy- Rahab is in the lineage of Christ in Matthew

Now this is what they would do they would have the shields that were made of laminated wood, w/ hardened leather and lined around the edges with metal.

These shields were capable to interlocking w/ other shields to form one big shield or moving wall.

The faith we are used to sitting in chairs, trains, planes, cars, only in things that faith is only as reliable as it was built to handle.

You can have faith all day and get ready to sit down in a chair that you know will not hold you up; and still fall.
(This faith somewhat shares with us what we think faith is; faith actually putting your full weight on God.)

Let me burst a bubble in here;

When we pray and say God right now, what we really say to God is that I don't have faith to rest in the fact that you know what's best and when it's best.

Somebody asks well, what is Faith?

Faith is being sure of what we hope for and certain of what we do not see.

faith is acting upon belief

Knowing that what you see is not what you get.

We use the term faith glibly or should I say loosely.

There are two types of faith, right here and we need to find out which one we have.

- A faith in our mind
- A faith in our heart

The difference is a faith in our mind says I can and I will
While the faith in our heart says I have and I do

Let me break it down even more.

You can be sick on your death bed and have a faith in your mind and say to everybody that comes to visit; I'm going to get better.

Still be sick and have faith in our heart and not even address the matter.

(Story of Father and little girl my head hurts; just say I am healed)
Let's say it like this have you ever know someone to say I'm going to be alright and be crying.

I hate to drop the bomb but that is not real faith; that's just mind faith.

When you have faith in your heart you know everything is going to be alright.

The kind of faith that Jesus had in the Garden of Gethsemane; whatever has to happened I know you know what you are doing; that's a shield of faith that I'm not going to let my guard down because I know whatever God decides to do he knows best.

Faith also means that you act upon what you know God is able to do. (Shadrach…)

Faith is building a ship on dry land and it hasn't rained for years
Faith is washing your face in a muddy river believing to cleanse your sickness
Faith is being told to carry the very bed you been laying on for 38 years
Faith is expecting water to pour out from a rock
Faith is believing that birds are going to be your waiters when you get hungry

Faith is putting all of your weight on God.
The Helmet of Salvation

      –   The Helmet was made of thick leather covered with meat l plates; some were made with molded metal.

      –   It guards your mind and your thoughts
If you get hit in your head you thinking is rattled, and shaken.

      –   If satan can get our minds to disbelieve what we heard, then he has our faith wavering and our heart in despair.
Many folks today are swept away because their beliefs are so weak they are persuaded by any and every one.

Cults
Compounds
Clicks

Zion ranch in West Texas
Where they had incest going on
Marrying at young ages
They believed everything they heard that man say

Jim Jones
David Koresh
In fact, let me say this Mormons and Jehovah Witness when you study boast on the fact that they convert more Baptists than anything.

When your mind is not protected by what you know, who you know, and where you are Spiritually you will listen and fall for anything.

When you know what you know what you know what you know then nobody can cause you to waver.

You see the helmet refers to the mind being controlled by God.

Watch this, the problem is many of know what we believe but we do not know why we believe what we believe.

I don't want to get too deep into the theology of this text and lose anybody but;

We believe in God, don't we?

But why do we believe in God.

We believe in his power, but why do we believe in his power.

We believe in salvation; but why do we believe in salvation.

We believe in the trilogy of God; but why do we believe in a triune God.

We believe in Heaven but why do we believe in Heaven.

It's deeper than what we think;

We believe but why?

That's where Jehovah Witnesses, Mormons, Catholicism, Jewish beliefs trap us.

We are adamant about what we believe but we are lost as to why we believe what we believe.

It's like this I believe that 4+4=8 but they only way I believe that is because I learned the math in order to calculate the problem.

I really don't know how far to go, but I do know we cannot have the helmet adequately put on if we do not know the why to what we believe.

Satan's goal is to cause us to lose heart b/c we cannot be certain of our beliefs.

We are in battle in our minds.
  - Romans 12:1

  - He says the only way transformation can come is by renewal.
    a. Otherwise I cannot change who I am until I see who I need to become.
    b. I don't know who I am to become until I see a snapshot in the scriptures.
    c. If I am to be like Jesus, I cannot just conjure a picture in my mind of what he may look like I have to see visually so that I might see the actual photo of my projection.

Somebody say to you I want you to look, act, and talk like Pastor Lyons; you could not do it if you have never seen me!

Are you with me?

  - You see renewal only comes through the study of God's word.
  - Satan is on the prowl going to and fro…

That's why the mind is so important to God because we become more confused when we do not keep our minds on him.

  - Men keep thinking they don't need women they can go with other men and be o.k.; God created me like this.
  - Women can be with each other because there are no good men left.
  - We do not need education
  - We do not have to be married to find intercourse- hiv
  - We can continue violence and feel good about it
  - I can gain more knowledge in jail than on the streets for free.

(Talking with my brother yesterday about young black men not in your family but in our family who are so institutionalized that it seems better to stay behind bars than to be free.

Satan is after our minds;

Salvation equips us with assurance.

If a man or woman has not been saved, he cannot have his mind protected from satan; everything is easily done.

Think about it if you think in your mind you are already defeated; all you are waiting for is the enemy to show up.

(Show at elimination Ant said let me go ahead and leave you are going to vote me off, they weren't even going to choose him until he said that.)

Have you ever watched a child put on a helmet they become unstoppable, and invincible because they think the helmet gives them so much power to hit anybody head on?

Job had on the helmet of salvation-

- His meat packing business had been shut down by the Sabeans
  Oxen and donkeys

- His wool and clothing line had been burned up by fire from up above
  Sheep and mutton

- His transportation business had been stolen by the Chaldeans
  Camels

- Your family heritage has just been erased by the winds
  Sons and daughters in the oldest boy's house-drinking and eating

How would you feel to have somebody come knocking on your door and saying everything you have is gone including your family; you need the helmet of Salvation.

Job's reaction was naked came I into…

He was still headed for more; he became sick…

Question: Is your armor tight enough to handle such a test as this?

He lost everything
His friends begin to accuse
He was sick
His wife wasn't comforting him

His helmet controls his thinking although he has been hit with a hard blow or blows.

That's why I said earlier you cannot expect to walk around without the helmet of Salvation and get hit in the mind or head Spiritually and sustain.

Your thoughts are discombobulated, messed up and misconstrued.

Listen to what the helmet produces even in heartache

Listen to his wife…
Though he slay me…

Because we know what we know and why we believe what we know.

That's how Job survived.

Romans 5:8, 9

Salvation means hope;

But not the hope we use every day.

We will say I hope it doesn't rain… and that statement has doubt in it already.

But if you were stranded without food for several days you could make it; but take away that hope and you will commit suicide or give up,

Think about those who are sick, they lose their hope to live.

We will be saved if we believe

But in order to genuinely believe we have to know why we believe what we believe.

A blow to the head at the right time in the right place can be fatal!!!!!!!!!!!!!!!

We can survive a broken arm, or a broken finger but a broken head is detrimental.

So let's protect our mind Spiritually by knowing what we know and why we believe what we know.

Sword of the Spirit

The sword used by the Roman Soldiers was 18" long and dual edged

The word is a powerful weapon
-Hebrews 4:12

This verse deals with the psychology of the word of God;

The psychology deals with the psyche or soul level we rarely ever talk about our soul.

It is the ability to reach into the pneuma, or Spirit of a man. Only the word of God can do this.

Only the word of God can discern the thoughts and intents of the heart; some of you might wonder why I always say I can tell who means me well and who doesn't this scripture right here slaps high five with Ephesians to solidify or back-up what I've said.

Two-edged sword- used offensively and defensively.

Psalms 119 is entirely devoted to this Sword of the Spirit.

- Let me quickly say many of us as I teach say amen to what you believe, but it is not our amen's that carry meaning, it is our obedience to what we have heard.

Many churches and Christians claim allegiance to the word of God, but preach with a closed Bible.

Otherwise we verbalize we believe it and follow it but will not open it for guidance.

Example:
Many people in their homes have the ten commandments hanging in their homes; but cannot recite 5 of them.

It was not by coincidence that when Jesus was tempted that the only thing he used was scripture.

We have to study the word; I know we are tired of hearing me say this, but study.
Don't just skim the surface and run with that, find out the deepest meaning of what you read.
II Timothy 2:15
Psalms 119:11
Don't just deceive yourself by hearing the word, put it into practice.
James

There is one person who you will never see in life.

Yourself- you see a reflection but you will never see yourself, the closest you could ever get is to look into the word and make yourself like Christ.

The sword is used for hand to hand combat.

You need to be very skillful in offense and defense.
If you are good at one and not the other somebody loses.

The term word here is not the usual translation as logos.
which refers to general statements or messages?

The term word translated here is rhema which refers to individual words or particular statements.

As in Romans 10:17

Let me see if I can make this plain to you the difference in Rhema and Logos.

Rhema is in particular
Logos is in general

You cannot use any scripture just picked at random to ward off the attacks of satan.

We have to use the appropriate scripture for the particular attack.

Logos is used in the opening verse in John 1:1

Then RHEMA means has a special application to an immediate situation.

The sword of the Sprit is the saying of God applied to a specific situation.

This is kind of when we read a scripture and the words come alive; has that ever happened, you feel powerful.

Looking for an answer and this scripture pops in our mind

In between a rock and hard place and a verse jump into our mind and we feel at ease.

Because the Spirit brings it to our remembrance.

Comes out of nowhere like a sword and slices the enemy.

I cannot be in a bind by the enemy and financially bankrupt and say but m God shall supply...

Because that scripture is not talking about everybody it is specifically talking about the preacher.
Philippians 4:19

It doesn't apply to everybody.

Matthew 4:4

Otherwise my priority is to please God first then to please myself.

Watch this;

Jesus did not defeat satan by knowing scriptures.

There's more to it than just knowing scriptures, Jesus defeated satan by knowing the word of God and being obedient, and knowing which scriptures to use.

If he had not been obedient and knew the word he would have easily been swayed.

Oswald Chambers said: "The only way you can truly trust God and love God is to obey Him"

You have to spend daily time in the scriptures in order to adequately know how to interpret and dissect the word of God.

It doesn't come in just listening to me, or watching it on television or coming to church; it come in personal time with Him.

Realize that the only way you can communicate with God is through scriptures that is His language.

Let's go back to II Timothy 2:15
- How can you show something that is not there?
- How can you be approved if you do not know what for?
- How can you rightly divide something you do not even read?
- Then he ends with the word of truth- well what did we say truth was a few weeks ago?

Intimately- I am aware of what she enjoys
Intellectually- I am aware of her thought patterns, I can't tell you what she is thinking but I am cognitively close.
Informatively- I am aware of what she likes for me to talk about.

- The word guides us

You have to know the word in order to fight off the enemy.

If you thinking about a man or woman who does not belong to you
"You have heard what I said if you look at a man or woman lustfully you have already committed adultery in his heart."

Fight the problem with the scriptures.

If you hate somebody
"If you hate your brother you have already committed murder"
If you are real serious about your sword; or bible study invest in it, not only read the bible but get reference books; concordances, commentaries, books that give history.

Because you cannot fight off the enemy with materials that you do not possess mentally and physically.

Praying always with all prayer and supplication in the Spirit, and watching thereunto with all perseverance and supplication for all saints.

Prayer is a solemn request, it is thanksgiving to God, please note this and remember for the end of this collection of lessons.

Let me expeditiously say that many people have not the full understanding of the Whole Armor of God based upon this single precept.

It's o.k. suit up
Dress up
Have the necessary equipment

But please note you cannot ascertain victory if you don't know the game plan.

I don't want you to allow this driving point to miss you out of the collection of these lessons.

There cannot be a win if you are not aware of the strategy.
You know many folk die in battle because they have the right stuff, but they forgot the objective.

Otherwise you can have the armor on, but either not know how to use or choose not to use it.

That's one thing but it is very depressing to have everything you need and didn't pay attention to the rules of engagement.

You see Paul makes a very valid point in these last few verses of instruction.

Listen how Pastor Paul places his plea;
Praying always with all prayer and supplication.

Now before we run to quickly, let us dissect those few words.

He says praying- all here should know whenever there is an ing on the end of any word it is a verbal action of its result.

Otherwise you do it redundantly, and you perform it with a result.

Watch this, he says praying always- which interjects that there should never be a time that you shouldn't pray.

I know your minds are running how can we pray all the time, someone asks?

I'm glad you asked!!!!!!!!!!

Remember prayer is a solemn request, and thanksgiving to God.

(Sometimes when I would do wrong my daddy would get mad at me and whip me or make me go to a room by myself and just stay there to think about it and If I asked to come out he would make me stay longer; we could have company over be at a family function anywhere but this was worse than a whipping to me because at least after the whipping I could go back and play with friends or family.)

This is the point I want to make;

When I came out sometimes I would go to my Daddy to get back in his good graces and say I'm sorry, and he would say don't be sorry just do what I ask of you.

God really says the same don't just be sorry show me in your living.

Otherwise live for me and your life will be a prayer; I will be satisfied with your thanking me through your lifestyle.
So prayer does not only come through kneeling down, it can and should come from your lifestyle, you can live a lifestyle of prayer.

The word always in Greek means in every season.

So one-point Pastor Paul was trying to hit home was and is that when you pray do not allow it to be in one season and not in another.

It's like this do not only pray while it's raining, pray when the sun is shining.

Sometimes in war, the situation calls for the most powerful weapon at your disposal. In this battle against the Spiritual forces of evil... in this battle we endure everyday- the most powerful weapon at our disposal, sadly, is often the weapon we pull out last... Prayer.

Now watch, even though Pastor Paul saves it for last in this list- he does so because it is the most important weapon of battle.
Not that it should be used as a last resort, or when all else fails, Christians are to always pray.
I Thess. 5:17

This is the foundational weapon of war.

We ought to think of prayer as a kind of Spiritual breathing, something we do naturally, almost without thinking about it.

Now Pastor Paul shifts a little and throws a different ingredient in this assemblage of armor.

He says now when you practice a lifestyle of prayer, pray in the Spirit.

Uhh ohh, there is where the sifter comes in to separate the over comers from the overcome.

It's like this whenever you live and pray do it in the Spirit, otherwise be led by the Spirit!

Well, what does he mean pray in the Spirit?

According to a survey; 90% of Americans pray in some regard.

Doctor M. E. Lyons

But just because one says he/she is praying, does not mean that they are speaking to God.

Just because someone sounds nice when they pray does not necessarily mean they have contact with God; but when their prayer pierces your spirit and creates an opportunity for God to show his power, that's when you know they are speaking to God.

To pray in the Spirit is to pray under the influence of the Spirit.
Ephesians 5:18

Live your life under and behind the Holy Spirit not anybody or anything!

We ought to be led by the Holy Spirit in our prayers; we do not practice this, but we ought to pray and ask God to give us what to say when we pray, especially for others. I do before counseling, altar prayer, etc.

God does not desire our lame repetitious, and redundant prayers.

Prayers that you memorized during childhood; tell Deja you are too old now to praying what you prayed at 5 talk to God!!!!

Your prayers should not be comprised of a wish list.
Give me this
Give me that.

Your prayers should be directed by the Holy Spirit.

Watch this, how do we really pray in the spirit?

I have an answer for you;
Romans 8: 26, 27

We really do not know what we ought to pray for the Spirit himself knows what to intercede for.

With groans that words cannot express.

He takes the hurts, tears, burdens, moans, groans, sighs, heart flutters and interprets them to God and explain what it is that we need.

When we do not know what to say the Spirit aids us in that area.

When we cannot find the words the Spirit helps us.

Have you ever been praying and get into your prayer, and start saying some things you didn't know you could put together it was because you were praying in the Spirit; and He took over.

Now Pastor Paul throws us a curve ball,

He says now that we know to pray, and how to pray, I need to tell you who to pray for.

For all Saints.

Not your choices, but all.

A-L-L

Now let us look at this scripture.
Matthew 5:44
Luke 6:28

Not against them but for them.

Not only should we pray for all saints, but we should pray for our Church; as a matter of fact, it should be a part of prayer every day.

Pastor the leaders
Hebrews 13:18

Then Pastor Paul moves toward the end and reminds us about the mindset to have.
Ephesians 3:1

He does not say a prisoner of Rome or Caesar, but to Christ.

He is in jail because of suiting up and preaching and teaching the word of God.
Otherwise we were ridiculed and scandalized for spreading the Word of God.

But listen to what he was praying for.

He did not pray for release.
He did not pray for a rescue.
He did not pray for protection.

He said pray also, otherwise after you pray for each other, don't forget to pray for me.

That I will be able to open my mouth, that words may be given to me so that I will be able to fearlessly make know the mystery of the Gospel.

Question:

What if we found ourselves imprisoned from our beliefs?
Would we still proclaim the Good News?

What if we found ourselves at the wrong end of a revolver?
Would we still proclaim the Gospel?

What if we found ourselves tortured for the sake of Christ?
Would we still speak the Word?

Then in the midst of imprisonment, in the shackles, braced with the chains; he closes and says Peace be to the brethren.

Peace means Shalom; he wishes the fullest of blessings of life and grace- to all who love Jesus with an undying love.

If your car is hydroplaning on the loop headed for a brick wall or oncoming traffic at 50 mph; what would you do?
I know; you would pray "Lord help me"

The doctor comes into your exam room with test results with a worried frown on his face; what do you do?
I know, you pray.

But what about when the sun is shining and the birds are chirping?
We take it for granted.

What about when we go to the Doctor's office and comes in smiling and says well everything looks good?
You leave happy but forgot to pray.

Pastor Paul leaves us here for a reason... this is a call to pray and make a lifestyle of it!

Not just to pray but pray powerfully.
To pray specifically
Pray constantly

Not just when the chips are down; not just when all else fails; when you don't have anywhere else to turn... but pray always/ in every season.

God is there waiting to have conversation with you to lighten your load in this war you are in.

Well let's end as we started what is prayer- it is a solemn request.

What is prayer?
It is Thanksgiving to God.

Don't be like I said I was come out of the room; or your situation and forget to live Thank you

To live I'm sorry instead of empty words.

Lesson Six

"Four Of A Kind; Trumps A Full House"
Mark 2: 1-12

<u>Introduction</u>:

- The issue we want to share in this lesson tonight is the tragedy of coming together with the right intended spirit.

- You see the problem of today is many are interested in coming to a place that is full or filling but their outside is raggedy.

- This particular scripture bursts with the epidemic of many placing a front on and not being truly sincere.

- You see because the record is this man was unable to walk and it really displays the spirit of selfishness in the text.

- Many come to church for the wrong reasons:

- To see what I can get out of the experience <u>(the reaction from his being there!)</u>
- To see what is going on in the church <u>(It was noised…)</u>
- To keep anyone else form coming in <u>(they would not budge in their stance)</u>

- They were following Jesus for what they could get out of Him.

I.   There is a principle that lies therein- Just because there is a full house: does not mean that the house is full of God!

       a.   Some were just glad for Jesus to be close to them. Nobody else will be able to say this like I can.

    1.   Understand this some folk pride themselves on being able to tell somebody yeah I was there when so and so happened.
    2.   I saw it with my own two eyes.
    3.   I heard him/her with my own two ears
    4.   Just satisfied being able to say how close Jesus was close to them; but had no idea it was supposed to be about; HOW CLOSE THEY WERE TO HIM!

       a.   You see when we are more concerned about ourselves than Him; we are simply glad just to have the word first than the word have us.
       b.   You see what brings you in might just b what keeps you....it was noised; which suggests that WORD ON THE STREET WAS...and some folk only come to Church for what they heard on the street.

    1.   <u>Gossip</u>
    2.   <u>Mess</u>
    3.   <u>Scandal</u>

- This story actually teaches us not to get so caught up in the hype; we miss the saving power of God.
- Some of them were full of pride.

II.   The four of a kind stopped the full house

       a.   The Word of God was Preaching the Word of God and when the FOUR OF A KINDS interrupted the Full House <u>EVERYTHING STOPPED!</u>

1. We allow liturgical order of Worship to trump the spirit; and it should be the other way around!
    a. Girl/Man, our Pastor did not even Preach Sunday morning and knows that is what is supposed to happen every Sunday morning and that is what we pay him to do.
    b. We had two altar calls; and that is too much praying
    c. This person does not look right so we should not allow them to do such and such.
    d. God does not operate in the same vain we do!
    e. SERVICE STOPPED; because there was a need

1. I am under the impression and belief that sometimes God will cause an interruption in service so that a need can be met.
2. Record has it that Jesus was in the middle of His <u>SERMON</u> and he put it on hold in order to address the interruption!

- Here they are cannot get in through the traditional route; so they said well let's use a contemporary route.
- Since you will not let us get to Him the normal way; we will go another way.
- You are so hell-bent on not letting us in because you got in first <u>(years/tenure)</u> we will do things our way.
- Their contemporary route got more attention than the traditional route; <u>WHY</u>? Because Jesus does not care how you get to him; just as long as you <u>GET TO HIM</u>!

1. <u>You may sing: I love the Lord He heard my cry and it move you; and I may sing Take me to the King and it move me…. both moves take us to the same place.</u>
2. <u>You may have a hard back Bible and I may read my Bible on my phone but both of them reveal the same Jesus.</u>
3. <u>You may love the Living Bible and I may love the Message Bible; both of them point and lift Jesus.</u>
4. <u>You may cry when you get happy and I may run and holler when I get happy; but we are happy about the same person.</u>

5. I may wear jeans and a t-shirt to Worship; you may wear Church suits to every service but the same changed heart in you is the same changed heart in me!

III.   Four of a Kind; HOW?

1. How are they FOUR OF A KIND? They are four of a kind first because they were more interested in getting the sinner to Jesus than sitting back and talking about him.
2. They were FOUR OF A KIND because they were determined to get him to Jesus no matter the cost?
3. They were FOUR OF A KIND because they didn't mind tearing things up; in order to build him up!

    a. Their hearts desire was to make sure he got to where Jesus was.
    b. How many friends around you; their first interest is to get you well; rather than themselves.
    c. True friendship is predicated and built on their propensity to help you before helping themselves.
    d. You see when we work together and use our individual gifts; we can get more people to Christ rather than trying to seek personal gains.
    e. If the four of them were seeking self-gratification; they would not have made it anywhere.

1. I am going to lead…no I am going to lead…I will let him down… no I will let him down…I want to be the one who is at the bottom to receive him so I can tell Jesus it was my idea…no each one of them did not care who received credit they just got it done.
2. Jesus response to the man was because of their faith…and their faith only intensified when their personal interests were set aside.
    –   I Peter 3:8: emphasis…but read to verse 12
    –   Philippians 2: 1-11

•   Get this; after the contemporary insert in Worship; THE PEOPLE LEFT AMAZED saying WE AINT NEVER SEEN NOTHING LIKE THIS.

- I think sometimes we are so closed minded we cannot accept the new wave God is trying to send our way!
- Our ways are not His ways; and our thoughts are not his thoughts... so saying: I don't think this is the way God would have this to be... can never be justified when there are positive outcomes!
  - Isaiah 55: 8-9

Lesson Seven

"One Minute"
Psalms 30:5

Introduction: Allow me to bring this story to home…

- Today somebody is still mourning and crying over past events.
- Have ever been so close to achieving a dream, yet it seems like you will never complete it and it does not matter how much closer you get to that dream; it seems like it farther and farther away.
- Or have you ever been so close to achieving a dream; and you watch it being crush right in your face.
- Have you ever had high expectations in someone, but your heart was broken because they fail to meet your expectations.
- Have you ever had so much hope in a love one or your child, yet they become an alcoholic or a crack head.
- It seems like you cannot keep them out of the streets or out of jail no matter what you do.
- Have you ever had someone to die who you loved dearly and they were your biggest inspiration in life?
- Have you ever been a Doctor's office and they say the Doctor will be with you in just one minute…?
- What about outside of a store and they open at nine but it is 8: 53…those minutes take forever…
- Or show up to work one minute late is no different than 10 minutes late…because late is late no matter how you look at it…I was a regional manager and upper management frowned on tardiness from any angle!

Notice that weeping…is predicated upon MAY…stop over, lodge, rest…

But joy (singing) is built on comes…a very authoritative form of the word COMES…

- Now get this the text says: NLT-joy comes with the morning…it's a byproduct of the morning…that's why they used to sing if you can just hold out till' the morning…everything will be alright!

- If we play close attention to the word play in this scripture, we can see exactly what David is saying…His anger is lasts only for a moment…a second…or a minute…you see because God's time is not our time…

- Our struggle comes out of the fact that we forget when we used to…if His time is not our time then why do we misconstrue this verse…

  a. Moment-regah-a wink-disturbance…now listen if we think like David we would agree…that God will repay whatever things that are good or evil…
  b. Then he says: but His favor is for life.

He really shares with us here tonight that we really do not know how long chronologically so weeping will last according to our watch…but we do know that joy cometh in the morning…

- One Minute enrolls us in Night School
  (Psalms 119:71)

- The writer here says…it was good for me to be in trouble… afflicted…suffering is just what I needed; because it TAUGHT ME to pay attention to your commandments…

  a. We know what it means to have difficulties show up…for some they never learn…others learn for a little while and then go back…but then are those who make an about face and allow it to make them the more strengthened…

- The death brought me closer to God
- The unemployment taught me to trust God more
- The separation taught me to love God first
- The rumors taught me to believe in His Word
- The children going astray taught me to leave it in His hands
- It taught me to believe his statutes…

Why would David use the word TAUGHT…I will tell you why because like they used to say; "The best lesson taught is the one that is bought!"

In our text for tonight David says when we are taught the most is in the night…you know when I was younger they used to have night school in high school

- the kids that came to school at night were serious, they were not there to play, horse around or anything else they were there for an education…

David teaches and shares an invaluable lesson that our nights are to keep us from playing around with God and pay attention to what His desire is; not ours!

So David was really saying your minute is not there to weaken us but to strengthen us…

Understand that David was known as a man after GOD's own heart; yet he is one of the biggest sinners in the Bible…

Understand that David committed many sins before his adulteress act with Bathsheba…

Before Bathsheba…David was a very arrogant man and he prided himself in war…

I'm going to let you in on a secret…shhh…I found this out in the course of my study of this text…

- The only reason we remain in the night is because we have not yet yielded to the word of GOD.

- There is a condition hinged on the door of this verse…weeping MAY endure for a night…now watch this; BUT

- Now we have established in the past that the word BUT is a transitional word, it is a word that says do an about face…

- Otherwise whatever you did or are doing; learn from it and then turn around so that joy can come…

James 1: 2,3- The only way to bring and usher joy in is welcome the night…I mean it's only a minute from night to morning…

You may be even going through a night of a bad relationship then making matters worse made the mistake of marrying them anyway because you thought that they could break a man and a woman…

It is evident that with God evening comes before morning…watch the imagery and significance of this scripture in all of our lives.
Genesis 1: 5, 8, 13, 19, 23, 31.

All the way through scripture in Genesis…we read: "The evening and the morning were the first day…" …" The evening and the morning was the second day".

In each of our lives we want to hurry and rush through the night time of our experiences…when it is the night times of our experiences that brings appreciation for the mornings of our joy!

- The shadows are scary…but truth is mornings do come…

- But notice it is on a continuum…night will come again…

But why do you think when speaking of being with Jesus; it is referenced to morning?

When the morning comes there will be no more sorrow, no more sadness, no more suffering, no more sickness...

<u>Closing Thought:</u>

We have no right to ask when sorrow comes, "Why did this happen to me?" unless we ask the same question for every moment of happiness that comes our way. ~Author Unknown

Lesson Eight

"Say What You Mean; And Mean What You Say!"
Matthew 7: 7-10

<u>The Message Bible:</u>
"Don't bargain with God. Be direct. Ask for what you need. This isn't a cat-and-mouse, hide-and-seek game we're in. If your child asks for bread, do you trick him with sawdust? If he asks for fish, do you scare him with a live snake on his plate? As bad as you are, you wouldn't think of such a thing. You're at least decent to your own children. So don't you think the God who conceived you in love will be even better?

Introduction: We find ourselves in many predicaments that prayer can fix; however, the problem is our prayers do not match up to what is in our hearts and minds!

Prayers with mere words will not make it very far if there is no belief in our communication…

We babble during our prayers and mean absolutely nothing and expect nothing in return…most of our prayers are redundant…same prayer every time…

- Askers are receivers. Seekers are finders. <u>Door knockers</u> are door-enterers.

I.   Powerful Prayers produce possibilities!

       Matthew 21:22-
       a. Prayer in this text means PROSS-U-KO-MY...be oratorical
           in worship...
I promise you this messed me up when I read the transliteration...it
actually means when you pray-you are worshipping-and when you are
worshipping-you are praying...

       b. Now what does this mean altogether- it simply means you
           can't even pray unless you worship...I know I have not been
           so far off...because I have felt in my spirit...that my prayer
           life has become better since I have been worshipping MORE!
       c. Get this: the word: BELIEVING means- PISS-TO-OH...
           which means credit!

   1. What is the purpose of credit?
   2. It is to get something with nothing.
   3. When you get a car on credit; you don't have the money you just
       pay it out
   4. Back in the days; you got food on credit
   5. You get a credit card; it means you can go shopping even when
       you are broke...BUT YOU HAVE TO PAY IT BACK AND
       MORE...stay with me...
   6. RECEIVE-means to forget...altogether it means when you
       worship-pray you will get what you want on credit but the fees
       will be forgotten...otherwise you don't owe anything on it!
   7. Your faith was the payment!

   –   If we expect our prayers to work; they must be full of faith and
       worship...if not, they are words without expectation or evidence!

II.   Pitiful prayers prevent His power!
       Luke 9: 37-43

When they came down off the mountain the next day, a big crowd was
there to meet them. A man called from out of the crowd, "Please, please,

Teacher, take a look at my son. He's my only child. Often a spirit seizes him. Suddenly he's screaming, thrown into convulsions, his mouth foaming. And then it beats him black-and-blue before it leaves. I asked your disciples to deliver him but they couldn't."

Jesus said, "What a generation! No sense of God! No focus to your lives! How many times do I have to go over these things? How much longer do I have to put up with this? Bring your son here."

While he was coming, the demon slammed him to the ground and threw him into convulsions. Jesus stepped in, ordered the vile spirit gone, healed the boy, and handed him back to his father. They all shook their heads in wonder, astonished at God's greatness, God's majestic greatness.

a. We often ask for those who really believe to come and pray with those who are seeking prayer…but if we do not believe or are doing it for show; it hinders the prayer…it is like have distortion on the line…

(Have you ever been on the phone and someone was saying something real important…but the distortion keeps you from hearing…nothing is wrong with the phone it is in the connection…)

b. Pope Pius XII said in the late 1800's- "A man without prayer is like a tree without roots." Then another person said "don't expect a thousand-dollar answer with a ten cent prayer…"

c. There must not be wavering in the prayer; there can be no disbelief on the line.

d. In this text Jesus asks the question: "How long have you been in Church and here it is you cannot pray and something take place for the little boy…"

e. I mean you have heard me pray; at least you ought to mimic what I have said and then place some belief in it…but NOTHING took place when you prayed…and the sad thing is THEY KNOW IT…one of the worst things in the world as a testimony is for those who are in Church with us…not desire for us to pray with and for them…the reason being is they KNOW and have SEEN your prayers DON'T WORK…

f. He also called them corrupt; WHY was my question...I know now...we are not representing HIM like we should!

III. You will be exposed through your prayers

    a. With every portion of this scripture there is positive on the other side of negative...

1. <u>Ask-Given</u>
    a. Now watch this: If we are to go by this scripture; it says WHATEVER it is that we ASK it SHALL be given...
    b. Otherwise, no matter what we ask God for it will be done... so the question here is are we sincerely praying to God...and then WHAT are we asking; whatever we ask ought to be in HIS will...

2. <u>Seek-Find</u>
    a. Seek is to worship...so Prayer is really three pronged...When we pray we ought to worship Him...when you worship Him... it should not be internal; worship is external...Worship is something that others should see you do towards God! Now don't get me wrong it can be private; but it ought to be public as well.
    b. Some do not feel comfortable with public worship because they have never spent time privately worshipping...
(You worship the ground they walk on...)

3. <u>Knock-Door Opened</u>
    a. <u>Why does a person knock on a door?</u>

1. In order that they might walk through it...
    a. Opportunities...Job, Relationships, Finances...

2. That you might ask someone out; through it...
    a. Problematic situations...come out of an abusive situation... depression...misery...salvation (Revelation 3:20...He is the

only one that will go in; we have to ask them out of that lifestyle…)

3. Offer something to the person on the other side of the door…
    a. Advice…praying that they would receive needful words of wisdom…direction…focus for their lives!

Closing: The most important part of prayer is not that we talk; but that we listen…because in the scripture Matthew 7:7 the most imperative statement that is given is FIND…how so; it is because we talk all the while and never ASK God to FIND His Will so we can receive what is ours!

We would much rather drop off our requests; and not even wait and see what He has to say…What is there for you to FIND at the end of your prayers…

- I pray and then FIND a quiet place to Hear…drive nowhere sometimes to just FIND His direction…No radio…Just me and God…THIS IS WORSHIP as well…

Lesson Nine

"A Giver That Cheerleads"
II Corinthians 9:7

Objective of a cheerleader is to do something physical or say something inspirational to either boosts your support or solicit your involvement in the event taking place.

Notice that a cheerleader does not stop cheering just because they are losing; it is then theirs to pull the morale of the fans out of the slump they are in.

God does not accept the gift that a person does not want to give.

There are three things that this verse shares with us that God expects from the giver in faith.

People who walk up to us; shun them away.

Churches have people come and we discourage them by sending them elsewhere.

The process not only works from the members to the church, and the church to them members but also the more so the church to the world.

The Jews had two chests for alms, or money, offerings.

One was necessary, what the law required, the other was free-will offerings.

The first nothing is said to do what the law required them to do, but of the second it says God loved them.

Think real hard on this we do what is required most of the time of us in our tithing, but in our free- will offering we does not love us.
The root word of purpose is pose! Hmm.

Wonder what that means.
To intend to give

Giving ought to originate in the heart not the mind.
(Expound)

Joy originates from feelings and feelings are birthed out of the heart so when God speaks to us, we learned last week he speaks to us in the pneuma which is our soul, now what joins the spiritual and the physical; it is the heart.

So if we are to give cheerfully it must come from our heart.

Example when we mess up or forget something we usually say charge it to my head not my heart, which signifies that our mind is incapable of keeping up with what we know we should do.

So it is with Giving by faith.

We ought not to leave it to our mind to give; it should be borne out of heart.

Many have it down pat what we are going to give every Sunday or every service; this is not giving in faith, because your heart never speaks the same way.
(Expound)

This is one of the reasons Jesus tells those Self-proclaimed Christians it is not what's in your mouth or on your minds I am concerned about;

You praise me with your lips but your hearts are far from me.
Matthew 15:8
Because when we give based upon our mind it is very much short of what we ought to do.
(That's why Paul says let this mind be in you...)

When Paul uses the word mind he uses the word mind to describe the heart, the viscera.

The words each one in Greek is masculine, which means it starts with the man; if the man does not want to give the house is already in shambles.

Watch the way the verse is really to be read in Greek this verse actually reads a cheerful giver God loves.

Which signifies that you have to love to give before God gives to the lover?

Now understand this verse does not say that God does not love the folk who do not gives, however it does say that he loves a cheerful giver.

It's like this I love everybody but when you are bent on giving me to me because of what I have done or because of how you feel about me out of your appreciation the more I want to do for you.

The word love here is not only that of a feeling but as God approves or he values.

Otherwise whoever loves to give God values, and a person you value you keep happy and joyful.

So if you hate to give, he disapproves you and does not value you, as if to say you are no benefit to the kingdom's cause.

Because lest you forget without faith it is impossible to please God.

I. The giver must give as he purposeth in his heart.

1. It does not mean that they cannot be encouraged to give, or that they ought not to be stirred to give.

   It means that the person is
   • To think about the need
     (Place your mind on the needs of the church and others, whether you know the specific needs or not, there are needs to be met)

   • To think about what to give sacrificially
   • (Not what I can spare- that's why it says sow sparingly, if you can spare $5 that is not giving bountifully)
   • To make a decision about what he should sacrifice in order to give what we should.
     (Not based upon the outcome, but based upon the income- otherwise that you have given the way you should have given, not with speculation in mind.)

   • To give exactly what he should give.
     (Not just because they ask for a certain amount)

II. The giver must not give grudgingly

   – not out of sorrow
     I could have used that money for something else

   – not with reluctance or regret
     Man I bet you they ain't going to do right with that money
     Man I sure hated to give that $100 that was all I had.

   – If you complain about the gift, then your gift has become displeasing to God.
     Pay attention right here I can help you if you allow me, it helped me; I have the anecdote on how to give.

Cheerful in Greek means hilarious- weird application isn't it.

But it really makes sense,

Whoever gives absolutely loves to gives so much that it puts joy so deep down in their heart that is where they find folly and fun.

III.   The giver must not give out of necessity

Your gift is not acceptable to God when they:

- Are forced to give
- Give because of what others will think
- Give to keep others from pestering him
- Give for personal honor and recognition

They are saying I have given this much to the church, and they won't even listen to what I have to say.

I helped to build this church
If it wasn't for me, we wouldn't be where we are.
Some have even say if it wasn't for you Pastor Lyons we would still be in the hole; not so if we would just learn how to sow bountifully we would reap bountifully.

Watch this bountiful in this text means a blessing- so in essence it really says whoever sows a blessing shall reap a blessing.
You know how you see on television folk running up while the preacher is preaching there are sowing in to the word that God has put in the mouth of the preacher. It's biblical.

But let's go a step further, it is also saying to anyone who is blessing us spiritually.

What God is really saying he will be no man's debtor; if you bless him, he cannot do anything but bless you.

Now watch how God works he is one that will not let the creation outdo the creator.

(Expound)

He is faithful to bless where we are faithful to obey.

He is not saying how much, but rather what to do with what we have.
We know.

II Corinthians chapter 8:12-15

IV.   Our attitude when we give is much more important than the amount we give.
(The woman and her mite)
Mark 12:41-44

- He is much more concerned about how we give from what we have.

- We ought to think and pray on what God wanted them to give.

Paul said I thought it necessary to talk about this to bring it to your attention, II Corinthians 9:5

He literally says you enjoy all of your grain by eating it, or lose some of it by sowing it, and later reaping a bountiful harvest.

Well let me appease your thoughts what is the money used for I am glad you asked- II Corinthians 9:12

- One Greek word derives from diakonia not diakonos that's deacon.

-service (official)
-minister
-aid need of saints

Question: Can a man be a loser of doing that which God is pleased?

Lesson Ten

"The Danger Of A Cover-Up"
I John 1:9/Proverbs 28:13

Introduction: Many folks have chiseled confessions...torn testimonies... altered admissions...they get rid of what they do not want to share...

We tell what we want to be told and stuff away all that we either feel ashamed of or are not going to ever admit that took place...because sometimes it is too embarrassing to admit we did it...

We will discuss in depth the severity and tragedy in attempting to cover up that which should be exposed...skeletons in our closet ought to be acknowledged to GOD and given away for good!

Let's look at I John 1: 5-7

Cover here means to conceal...clothe...otherwise make dress the sin up so others will look at the clothes rather than the sins...

Beloved Solomon was the wisest man outside of God...he says YOU WILL NOT PROSPER...first thing is prospering means <u>SAH-LOCK</u>...to make any progress...succeed...be profitable...

It's like this as long as you are lying to yourself and to God...you will only go as far as your confession will allow you...

- It's kind of like a dog that has a chain on

Beloved confession is the chain that keeps us from getting to what it is we desire to get in life…it looses us from the chain…but it shortens the chain of the enemy

It is inevitable we will sin…there is no escaping sin…it is innate…it is a part of who we are…or should I say who we have become since the beginning of time!

In this lesson Solomon teaches us that two things can be done as it relates to our sins…

Concealing- you see concealing on builds a wall between us and God… because when we attempt to hide that which He already knows it causes Him to hide His face from us.

Amnesia produces arrogance…

— Well, what does that mean to me…if He is hiding from you; you feel as if when you need Him there is no answer that is only because His thoughts are…why help you when you won't be honest with Him…?

— Think about it…when someone is not honest with us; we are reluctant to help because honesty will breed help…

(M.I.B-III…Will Smith-Agent J…went back in time to help Agent K-Tommy Lee Jones and Agent K would not help Agent J until he was totally honest with him…)

You do know that concealed sin will only eat away at us…because if we are saved…we know when we are wrong; but to not acknowledge it and fix it…it becomes embedded in us and in our minds to a place whereas we overlook others sin and accept it because we have concealed our own…

(The woman CAUGHT in the very act...John 8: 1-11)

- [3-6] The religion scholars and Pharisees led in a woman who had been caught in an act of adultery. They stood her in plain sight of everyone and said, "Teacher, this woman was caught red-handed in the act of adultery. Moses, in the Law, gives orders to stone such persons. What do you say?" They were trying to trap him into saying something incriminating so they could bring charges against him. [6-8]Jesus bent down and wrote with his finger in the dirt. They kept at him, badgering him. He straightened up and said, "The sinless one among you, go first: Throw the stone." Bending down again, he wrote some more in the dirt. [9-10]Hearing that, they walked away, one after another, beginning with the oldest. The woman was left alone. Jesus stood up and spoke to her. "Woman, where are they? Does no one condemn you?" [11] "No one, Master." "Neither do I," said Jesus. "Go on your way. From now on, don't sin."

Now get this...I have never seen this before...HE ASKS A QUESTIONS YOU THAT HAVE NO SIN THROW ONE... (A ROCK) a=stay with me...they caught her the message Bible says red-handed...and He throws the pressure back on them...the one of you who has not done anything you are welcome to cast a stone...

Do you know why they left?

It was not because they had sinned alone...
It was not because Jesus was the one asking...

It was because when you conceal sin; you need to be confronted sometimes that you have been guilty of the very same thing...

And when you conceal and suppress a thing you go about logically thinking you have never done it; because first thing is YOU WERE NEVER CAUGHT...

People love pointing fingers at people who have been caught; but forget the only difference between them and you are that we have not been caught!

<u>Confession-</u> God has built in the believer a divine alarm system that will alert us when we go astray and that is our conscience…and many times we ignore the alarm…

*It will not be hidden…Jeremiah 2:22-There is nothing that can COVER UP…what He desires to be shown…

- <u>Message Bible: Scrub, using the strongest soaps.</u>
  <u>Scour your skin raw.</u>
  <u>The sin-grease won't come out. I can't stand to even look at you!"</u>

• Guilt can have a devastating effect upon our mental and emotional state…

• Psalm 32:3-4, "When I kept silent about my sin, my body wasted away through my groaning all day long. For day and night Thy hand was heavy upon me; my vitality was drained away as with the fever heat of summer. Selah."

This is when David was confronted by Nathan…sometimes you have to look in the mirror and see yourself…

- David experienced guilt-induced anxiety and depression when he tried to 'conceal' his sin from God. Not only did he feel the emotional and mental misery, but he experienced the physical effects as well: Psalms 51:10…

Message Bible reads like this:

7-15 Soak me in your laundry and I'll come out clean,
    scrub me and I'll have a snow-white life.
Tune me in to foot-tapping songs,
    set these once-broken bones to dancing.
Don't look too close for blemishes,

give me a clean bill of health.
God, make a fresh start in me,
    shape a Genesis week from the chaos of my life.
Don't throw me out with the trash,
    or fail to breathe holiness in me.
Bring me back from gray exile,
    put a fresh wind in my sails!
Give me a job teaching rebels your ways
    so the lost can find their way home.
Commute my death sentence, God, my salvation God,
    and I'll sing anthems to your life-giving ways.
Unbutton my lips, dear God;
    I'll let loose with your praise.

Psalm 38:3-8, 17-18, "There is no soundness in my flesh because of thine indignation; there is no health in my bones because of my sin. For my iniquities are gone over my head; as a heavy burden they weigh too much for me. My wounds grow foul and fester. Because of my folly, I am bent over and greatly bowed down; I go mourning all day long. For my loins are filled with burning; and there is no soundness in my flesh. I am benumbed and badly crushed; I groan because of the agitation of my heart...For I am ready to fall, and my sorrow is continually before me. For I confess my iniquity; I am full of anxiety because of my sin."

I was reading a book written by that great mind: Sigmund Freud...he speaks about the id, ego, and superego...

These three house the conscious...preconscious...and unconscious...

Conscious houses (the tip of the iceberg) ...name...address...number...age...

Preconscious houses (water around the tip of iceberg) ...what you watched last night...what you ate last week...

Unconscious houses (iceberg that is massive under the surface of the water) ...painful memories...conflict...wrongdoings...

What happens when we sin for some they file it away in the unconscious and it becomes too massive to fit in the space it is supposed to be and not removed it moves into other areas...now it forces itself on the conscious... it no longer is wrong...

Suppression will turn to Depression...Depression will turn to Obsession... Obsession will turn into Exception...Anything goes...it is ok now... Do you know how many ships have sunk because of what lies underneath?

Now I did not tell you what else prosper means in this particular text Proverbs 28:13...TO PUSH FORWARD...BREAK OUT...GO OVER...

So when we are transparently honest with GOD He will PUSH us into things we only dreamed about...

He will cause us to BREAK OUT of situations we were caught in...

Then He will strengthen us to GO OVER...that which we were struggling to climb...but it only happens when we CONFESS...

But we must not only confess...we must FORSAKE THEM...
  – Meaning...to leave them...let alone...neglect...
(It's like ignoring a person; you know they are there, but you act like they aren't...)

Closing thought: Jesus is hanging there on the cross between two thieves... both are speaking bad to Jesus...and then Jesus bows and prays...FATHER FORGIVE THEM...and then one thief changes...and says:

We deserve to be here; He doesn't
We deserve to die; Jesus does not
Hush he says to the other thief...remember me when thou come into thy Kingdom...

You missed it; the man has not even confessed of his wrongdoing until now...

Jesus sees a naked man; NO CHARADES...and says TODAY thou wilt be with me in Paradise...

Why do you think the thief's prayer was answered...because he was transparently honest of what he had done and who he was...?

Lesson Eleven

"The Secret To Having A Happy And Blessed Church"
Revelation 1: 1-20

Introduction:

- Who wrote the book of Revelation? Was it John the Baptist? Was it John the beloved disciple? It was John the beloved the disciple who is also known as John the Revelator; the writing style is similar to suggest that he was the author.

- FYI: John actually wrote more verses and letters than Paul!

- This book was written while John was on the isle of Patmos.

- The word Revelation itself means: Apokalupsis; which means unveiling; which derives from Apocalypse. It is actually the grand central stations where all other sixty-five books come into the station.

- If we feel like things are bad now; think about after the removal of the church.

- I am going to throw you a great nugget early on...Understand that this is the only book in the Bible whereas the reader is blessed by merely reading it and then keeping its statutes. But most importantly READING IT! It is to be read in Church because there is a blessing in it.

- We are blessed when we read the Word! (<u>I Timothy 4:13</u>) Paul was telling Timothy the very same thing keeps on reading; read for teaching sake, read for Preaching sake, but also read for witnessing sake…this is the issue we have no one wants to witness; our main priority is to READ to SHARE!
- This book repeatedly makes reference to three times: past, present and future! That is why it is quite important to know the seven dispensations. <u>(This is not an easy task; to utilize all the necessary tools to understand the Revelation but if you desire to be blessed it is necessary!)</u>

– Many frown on the use of Greek and Hebrew but here in the book of Revelation He actually says I am Greek!
– He says I am Alpha and Omega…and when He says that His Words are filtered through the Angel- AN-GUUL-OSS. He says in Greek Alpha; Nu; Gamma; Eta; Lambda. It means to watch over; Pastor, messenger.
– When we speak of happiness; this book actually points to those of us who are saved to learn to be happy off of the gleanings of this book!

- Happiness is a very elusive concept and many will never find it; pursuing the things they pursue because one writer says if a person is happy and moves a few inches the happiness is subject to be lost.
- Happiness should come also because we should know that our Savior is on the throne.
- This book of Revelation is a peculiar book and it is somewhat odd that a book that many are deathly afraid of begins with the word blessed!
- This book of Revelation was written to educate and enlighten us to be better as a Church.
- You mean to tell me that a book full of prophecy (what shall come to pass), apocalyptic (complete destruction of the world), and epistolary (writing of letters as a novel) material can be so joyful and happy? Yes, this book is actually engaging to encourage us to be blessed and not cursed.

- Matthew 13:37- we cannot approach Ministry or anything spiritual using our physical means we must operate in the spirit man...here what the spirit saith to the Church.

– The first rapture Christ's feet will never have touched the ground; but at the second rapture they will touch down...I Thessalonians 4: 16, 17-Not touch...Zechariah 14: 4, 5-they shall touch: REVELATION 14:1!

– Seven is used over and over again in this book: it is the number of completion; perfection...there are seven days in a week, there are seven noted in an octave, there are seven primary colors. Seven is used as completion.

It actually has forty-nine sevens listed in Revelation which is seven –sevens and that equal forty-nine!

The rapture should never be confused with the second coming of Christ!

– <u>One of the misunderstandings is: When will the rapture take place? Will it take place before the time of Tribulation? PRE-TRIB. Will it take place in the middle of the Tribulation? MID-TRIB. Or will it take place after the Tribulation? POST-TRIB. The question has been raised because of those wanting to know if the saints have to endure the suffering (Tribulation) at all. WE WILL BE CAUGHT UP!</u>

- Any questions about Revelation so that we might look into answering any questions for our upcoming sessions concerning Revelation?

-HANDBOOK TO BE GIVEN OUT TO THE STUDNETS-

-Chart of Facts-

COMPLETION AND CIRLCE OF BIBLICAL TRUTHS

IN GENESIS WE FIND	IN REVELATION WE BEHOLD
1. The beginning of time 1:1	Time no more
2. The beginning in Paradise	The wonderful Paradise to come
3. The creation of the Heavens and the Earth 1:1	The New Heaven and the New Earth 21:1
4. The beginning of morning and evening 1:3-5	No night in the New Jerusalem 22:5
5. Paradise lost 3: 22-24	Paradise restored 2:7, 22: 1, 2
6. The tree of life, and the way to it guarded. 2:9, 3:24	The tree of life, with man permitted to partake of its fruit. 22:2
7. The river going out from Eden 2:10	The river of water of life, flowing out of the throne of God. 22:1
8. Man is made steward over the Garden of Eden. 2: 15	Man being made a kingdom and priests who reign. 5:10, 20:6
9. We are told that man shall surely die. 3:17	No more death. 21: 3,4
10. The narrative going form life to death.	The narrative going from death to life.
11. The first bride was taken from the wounded side of the first Adam. 2:21	The second bride, the Church (21:9) taken from the wounded side of the second Adam.
12. The first was performed by God in the presence of the angels.	The last wedding performed by God in the presence of redeemed saints. 19:9

13. The serpent entered the world. 3: 1-4	The serpent being cast down out of the world. 20:10
14. The Word of God was added to. 3:4; cf 3:3 with 2:17	Divine judgment being added to those who add to God's Word. 22:18
15. Man hid himself because of sin. 3:8	Men hiding themselves because of sin. 6: 14-16
16. The pronouncement of a four-fold curse. 3: 14-19	There will be no more curse. 22:3
17. God clothed man in skins of animals-typifying the blood of Christ. 3:21	God clothes man in clean linen made white by the blood of the Lamb. 7:14, 19:8
18. The first Adam was defeated by Satan. 3: 22-24	The second Adam was victorious. 20:10
19. Human beings losing a chance to eat of the tree of life. 3: 22-24	Humankind yet eating of that tree. 22:2
20. A garden becomes a wilderness.	A wilderness becomes a garden.
21. We read the sacrifice of the first lamb. 3:21	We see the Lamb standing victorious on Mount Zion. 14:1
22. Man's punishment was greater than he could bear. 4:13	The punishment of the wicked will be great, 21:8, but for the righteous there will be no punishment. 21:4, 20: 4-6
23. Man wept for the first time. 27:34, cf. Hebrew 12:17	A time when no man sheds n more tears. 21: 3,4
24. The earth destroyed by a universal judgment. 6:1-8:22	The earth made new by a universal judgment. 21:1
25. The beginning of Babylon, which means confusion. 10:10	The destruction of Babylon, destruction of confusion. Chapter 18
26. Humanity's first rebellion against God. Chapters 3-4	An end to humanity's rebellion against God.

27. The first murderer, drunkard and rebel.	A city where nothing impure will ever enter it, nor will anyone who does what is shameful or deceitful, but only those whose manes are written in the Lamb's book of life. 21:27
28. The first physical death. 4:8	Promise of no more death. 21:4
29. The beginning of the curse. 3:15-18	The curse lifted. 22:3
30. The prophecy. Satan's head will be bruised. 3:15	The fulfillment: Satan is bruised and defeated. 19:20
31. The unveiling of Satan. 3:1, 14, 15	The unveiling of Jesus Christ. 1:1

The Book of Revelation-Facts

Introduction: This book is perhaps one of the most confusing and perplexing and misinterpreted books in the whole canon of the Bible. There are a multiplicity of teachers and Preachers who avoid studying and Preaching and teaching from it due to the in depth meanings and the codes that it speaks to us in on many occasions. This book is known to use apocalyptic dialogue and imagery that is quite intimidating and couples itself with prophecy to create a heightened awareness of what is to come. We will venture to see how important and pertinent it is to not avoid this book with all of the riches that lie therein for our benefit. The book of Revelation cannot be afforded to be ignored. Happy digging (studying and learning)!

Revelation Unfolded

1. The value of searching the Revelation
2. Who authored the Revelation?
3. The uniqueness of the book of the Revelation
4. The necessity for the Revelation
5. The structure of the Revelation
6. The message of THE Revelation

Items needing attention in the searching of the Revelation

1. Dispensations
2. The Rapture
3. The Tribulation
4. The Millennium: The contrast between the Millennium and the Second Coming
   - Post-millennialism
   - Pre-millennialism
   - Amillennialism

"The Things Which Were" (Chapter 1)

1. The Preamble (verses 1-3)
2. The Epistolary Greeting (verse 4-5a)
3. The Praise (verses 5b-8)
4. The Messenger's Vision: "In the Spirit, on the Lord's Day" (verses 9-20)

"The Things Which Are" (Chapters 2-3)

1. Seven Letters to Seven Churches
2. Why these Churches? They are used universally
3. The structure of the seven Messages
4. Past Context/Current Context and Application

"The Things Which Shall Be"/The Prophecy of the Revelation (Chapters 4-20)

1. John's Heavenly Vision
   a. After This-Rapture and Tribulation
   b. The Throne Scene

2. Reading the Prophecy
   a. Theologically given: Love and Judgment
   b. Structure in the Prophecy

3. The Tribulation Part One
   a. Seven Seals
   b. Seven Trumpets

4. God's Enemies depicted
   a. The Dragon (12: 1-17)
   b. The Sea Beast and Land Beast (13: 1-18)
   c. Babylon the Harlot (14: 1-20)

5. The Tribulation Part Two and the demise of God's enemies
   a. The Seven Bowls of Wrath
   b. The Destruction of Babylon
   c. The Destruction of the Beasts
   d. The Destruction of the Dragon

"The Things Which Shall Be"/The Promise of the Resurrection (Chapters 21-22)

   a. The New Heaven, The New Earth, The New Jerusalem
   b. Conclusion and Doxology

INNOCENCE

This dispensation extends from the creation of Adam in Genesis 2:7 to the expulsion from Eden. Adam created innocent and ignorant of good and evil, was placed in the Garden of Eden with his wife, Eve, and put under responsibility to abstain from the fruit of the tree of the knowledge of good and evil. The dispensation of innocence resulted in the first failure of man, and in its far-reaching effects, the most disastrous. It closed in judgment: "So he drove out the man." See Gen. 1:26; Gen. 2:16, 17; Gen. 3:6; Gen. 3:22-24.)

CONSCIENCE

By the fall, Adam and Eve acquired and transmitted to the race the knowledge of good and evil. This gave conscience a basis for right moral judgment, and hence the race came under this measure of responsibility-to do good and eschew evil. The result of the dispensation of conscience, from Eden to the flood (while there was no institution of government and of law), was that "all flesh had corrupted his way on the earth," that "the wickedness of man was great in the earth, and that every imagination of the thoughts of his heart was only evil continually," and God closed the second testing of the natural man with judgment: the flood. See Gen. 3:7, 22; Gen. 6:5, 11-12; Gen. 7:11-12, 23.)

HUMAN GOVERNMENT
Out of the fearful judgment of the flood God saved eight persons, to whom, after the waters were assuaged, He gave the purified earth with ample power to govern it. This, Noah and his descendants were responsible to do. The dispensation of human government resulted, upon the plain of Shinar, in the impious attempt to become independent of God and closed in judgment: the confusion of tongues. (See Gen. 9: 1, 2; Gen. 11: 1-4; Gen. 11:5-8.)

PROMISE
Out of the dispersed descendants of the builders of Babel, God called one man, Abram, with whom He enters into covenant. Some of the promises to Abram and his descendants were purely gracious and unconditional. These either have been or will yet be literally fulfilled. Other promises were conditional upon the faithfulness and obedience of the Israelites. Every one of these conditions was violated, and the dispensation of promise resulted in the failure of Israel and closed in the judgment of bondage in Egypt.

The book of Genesis, which opens with the sublime words, "In the beginning God created," closes with, "In a coffin in Egypt." (See Gen. 12:1-3; Gen. 13:14-17; Gen. 15:5; Gen. 26:3; Gen. 28:12-13; Exod. 1: 13-14.)

LAW
Again the grace of God came to the help of helpless man and redeemed the chosen people out of the hand of the oppressor. In the wilderness of Sinai, He proposed to them the covenant of law. Instead of humbly pleading for a continued relation of grace, they presumptuously answered: "All that the Lord hath spoken we will do." The history of Israel in the wilderness and in the land is one long record of flagrant, persistent violation of the law,

and at last, after multiplied warnings, God closed the testing of man by law in judgment: first Israel, and then Judah, were driven out of the land into a dispersion which still continues. A feeble remnant returned under Ezra and Nehemiah, of which, in due time, Christ came: "Born of a woman-made under the law." Both Jews and Gentiles conspired to crucify Him. (See Exod. 19:1-8; 2 Kings 17:1-18; 2 Kings 25: 1 -11; Acts 2:22-23; Acts 7:5152; Rom. 3:19-20; Rom. 10:5; Gal. 3: 10.)

GRACE
The sacrificial death of the Lord Jesus Christ introduced the dispensation of pure grace, which means undeserved favor, or God giving righteousness, instead of God requiring righteousness, as under law. Salvation, perfect and eternal, is now freely offered to Jew and Gentile upon the acknowledgment of sin, or repentance, with faith in Christ.

"Jesus answered and said unto them, this is the work of God, that ye believe on him whom he hath sent" (John 6:29). "Verily, verily, I say unto you, He that believeth on me hath everlasting life" (John 6:47). "Verily, verily, I say unto you, He that heareth my word, and believeth on him that sent me, hath everlasting life, and shall not come into condemnation; but is passed from death unto life." (John 5:24). "My sheep hear my voice, and I know them, and they follow me: and I give unto them eternal life; and they shall never perish" (John 10:27-28). "For by grace are ye saved through faith; and that not of yourselves: it is the gift of God: Not of works, lest any man should boast" (Eph. 2:8-9).

The predicted result of this testing of man under grace is judgment upon an unbelieving world and an apostate church. (See Luke 17:26-30; Luke 18:8; 2 Thess. 2:7-12; Rev. 3:15-16.)

The first event in the closing of this dispensation will be the descent of the Lord from heaven, when sleeping saints will be raised and, together with believers then living, caught up "to meet the Lord in the air: and so shall we ever be with the Lord" (I Thess. 4:16-17). Then follows the brief period called "the great tribulation." (See Jer. 30:5-7; Dan. 12:1; Zeph. 1:15-18; Matt. 24:21-22.)

After this the personal return of the Lord to the earth in power and great glory occurs, and the judgments which introduce the seventh, and last dispensation. (See Matt. 25:31-46 and Matt. 24:29- 30.)

KINGDOM

After the purifying judgments which attend the personal return of Christ to the earth, He will reign over restored Israel and over the earth for one thousand years. This is the period commonly called the millennium. The seat of His power will be Jerusalem, and the saints, including the saved of the dispensation of grace, namely the church, will be associated with Him in His glory. (See Isa. 2:1-4; Isa. 11; Acts 15:14-17; Rev. 19:11-21; Rev. 20:1-6.

But when Satan is "loosed a little season," he finds the natural heart as prone to evil as ever, and easily gathers the nations to battle against the Lord and His saints, and this last dispensation closes, like all the others, in judgment. The great white throne is set, the wicked dead are raised and finally judged, and then come the "new heaven and a new earth." Eternity is begun. (See Rev. 20:3, 7-15; Rev. 21 and 22.)

START HERE (Homework Assignment- write down as many things that you can find in scripture that are in Heaven and as many things that are in Hell that you can find in scripture in Revelation.)

<u>Can anyone tell me what they received out of their reading assignment chapters two and three?</u>

- Four epistles are contained in <u>chapter 2</u>, and three in <u>chapter 3</u>.
- In the last four epistles the closing promise is placed <u>after</u> the injunction to "hear what the Spirit,"
- In the first three epistles the promise is <u>before</u> the injunction.

- The city of Ephesus was the capital of the Roman province of Asia.
- Ephesus is where Paul stayed for three years (Acts 19: 1-10, Acts 20: 17-38)
- Aquila and Priscilla and Apollos worked and labored.
- Timothy penned I and II Timothy; great Preaching went on here.
- Sixty miles from Patmos

He begins this epistolary letter to this Particular Church mentioning His place and mindset regarding the Church.

- <u>Seven stars in his right hand.</u>
  a. Stars represent the Ministers/Pastors

- <u>Lamp stands represent the Churches</u>
  a. Ephesus and etc., it actually speaks of the Churches in a universal manner.
  b. So it actually states that He walked in the midst of the Church with the Pastors in His right hand.

- Now understand that His right hand is the hand of Strength and Power.

1. Jesus is seated on God's right hand (Ephesians 1: 19-21)
2. Psalms 110:1
3. Psalms 118:16

4. Matthew 22:44
5. This <u>IN HIS RIGHT HAND</u> actually signifies that we are not only <u>IN</u> His right hand but in Him who is <u>AT</u> His right hand!

This statement signifies that He will protect His Ministers; now we must understand that in His proclamation here He is speaking of false teachers/Preachers but for those who are His…He WILL PROTECT THEM! This is why He calls them His angels.

- Those whom we <u>KNOW</u> are false teachers and Preachers He commends them for endures and not adheres to their false teachings.
- Notice here the reality of their being commended is that they had examined and discovered.
- Now a person can never discover or examine anything without research; the research and discovery spoken about here is to study themselves.
- He simply says that in order to know a person is incorrect in their leadership is to study for <u>YOURSELF</u> and not go on others understandings alone.
- He actually suggests that in order for the Church to be blessed they <u>MUST</u> adhere to the leadership and guidance of the angel; and the only ONE way to do that and be blessed is to <u>READ IT FOR YOURSELF</u>!
- But notice the fire He still sets underneath them and us. He says <u>BUT YOU NEVER QUIT! YOU NEVER FAINTED!</u>
- Even when you have found out otherwise about false teachers it does not relieve you for doing what is right because <u>HE HOLDS THEM IN HIS RIGHT HAND</u>!

You see in Revelation 1:13; God…He was simply seen in the midst, but in this chapter He is <u>WALKING</u> in the midst.

This implication teaches us that He now has to exact continuous supervision. He went from one to the next inspecting the lamp stands.

This was about the Church enduring the false teachings and teachers…but there is no way to do this if we do not read the Word; and thereby being blessed by reading Revelation.

Some people rebel and do not read because of who says it and their mindset of being their own boss and man/woman.

- This actually references the synoptic Gospels because in His First Advent He came seeking fruit and found none. The love that He knew was there was not evident! Neither was it visible.

Even with the reference to Jesus' eyes, and kneecaps, and hair and other things; we sometimes become caught up in the wrong things and cannot see the forest for the trees!

This is not a physical reference but a character reference.

This does not reference about who he is rather than what he stands for. Do you remember when his family showed up to church and called him out; that was his family many would say that who he is; but he was all about what he stood for…those who do my will!

Hair white wool-purity sinless-Glory
Eyes fire- judgment- he sees everywhere and everything and anywhere
Feet like fine brass or bronze- strength and perseverance
Gospel of peace
Voice like many waters- symbolizes authority, can thunder and comfort

I know thy works; implies that whether you really believe it or not; EVERYTHING that we do; seen and what we feel like unseen. HE KNOWS!

He complimented them before admonishing them.

The phrase somewhat against actually means OPPOSITION…it means PRIVATE!

In other words, you portray loving me when we are around friends.
You act like you love me when we are at Church
You seem as if you love me when it is to your advantage

- But at home you show me the true side.
- You do not speak to me at home
- We do not have pillow talk
- We do not even rest in the same bed. As a matter of fact, you don't even mention me when you lay down

You see because when you first fall in love with someone:

- You call all the time
- You cannot stand to be away from them
- You will even call and just hold the phone
- You will leave love letters in various paces
- You will sporadically buy gifts
- You will give them your last

- <u>Nothing but the fervent love of the Bride can satisfy the groom.</u>

<u>They had been at a height of excellence. 2. They had fallen from that height; there had been a spiritual declension.</u>

<u>When you leave your first love; to remove the candlestick would be to suffer the church to cease to exist.</u>

The light was in the <u>MIDST</u>-middle of them…if He is not in the MIDST THE LAMP <u>CANNOT BEAR LIGHT</u>. (Light needs to be centrally located)

He has the power to CONTINUE or REMOVE the Ministry depending upon our Hearing what the Spirit is saying to the church through the angel!

He has absolute control over Ministry.

These Church at Ephesus had become very harsh and self-satisfying because of their disobedience.

Nicolaiatans-Nicolaus are meant who taught that Christian liberty meant license to commit sensual sins.

Now get this Nicolas was one of the first seven diaconate ordained by the apostles. (Acts 6: 1-5; emphasis on 5)
These people who followed Nicolas led lives of unrestrained indulgence. They followed the wrong person and ended up being labeled here in Revelation.

He was converted from Judaism.
He allowed other men to marry his wife.
He believed in polygamy.

The prefix Nico means victory and laos meaning laity…when compounded it means victory of the lay people.

His only goal in Ministry was to have victory and power over those he should have had no power of.
Things found in Heaven and Hell according to the Book of Revelation

Heaven
  - Door being opened Revelation 4:1
  - Throne 4:2
  - Rainbow 4:3
  - 24 seats 4:4
  - Seven lamps of fire 4:5
  - Sea of glass 4:6
  - Four beasts with eyes in the front and back 4:6
  - Book with seven seals 5:1
  - A lamb with seven horns and seven eyes 5:6
  - Harps and golden vials full of odours; which are the prayers 5:8
  - White horse 6:2
  - Red horse 6:4
  - Black horse 6:5

- Pale horse 6:8
- White robe 6:11
- Golden censer 8:3
- Pregnant woman 12:2
- Red dragon with seven heads and ten horns 12:3
- War with the angels and the dragon 12:7
- Thigh print 19:16 (tattoo...we will discuss it more when we get to this lesson)
- Twelve gates 21:12
- Twelve foundations 21:14
- Golden reed 21:15
- Jasper wall 21:18
- City of gold 21: 18
- Precious stones 21:19
- Pearls 21:21

Hell

- Smoke 9:2
- Locusts 9:3 they had power like scorpions; they were commanded not to hurt the grass of the earth, nor any green thing but every man that hath not the seal upon their foreheads for five months not kill them; continuous stinging; they want to die but cannot... they were shaped like horses; had faces like men; hair like women; teeth like lion's tails like scorpions, 9: 7-10
- Fire and brimstone 20:10
- Great white throne 20:11
- Book of life 20:12

Revelation 2: 8 -11

This Church was under attack in her community and by city officials.

They held their own; they stayed true to Christ.
This one of the Churches Christ did not have to warn!

This really teaches us that the Angel ought to be the first to stand against persecution of the Church.

- Gay Marriage
- Poor
- Economy
- Distilleries
- Unemployment
- Adultery
- Fornication
- Misuse of Power

The word Smyrna means bitter!
It received its name from myrrh; this is the same ingredients to give Jesus drink on the cross! It is like a gum resin from a tree.

It made perfume and embalming fluid. Used to dull pain.

So this Churches name literally meant to dull the pain!

DO you know what alcohol and drugs were created to do; dull the pain? Most use them to deal with their bitterness and pain that is felt on the outside!

Think about the world.

- Divided
- Mass Shootings
- Parent/Child Killings
- Divorce at an all-time high

The church is taking pain pills; to dull the pain and not have to address it and just live with it!

Why you might ask is this happening; it is simple; because the angels will not stand up!

- As long as it does not directly affect my Church I'm ok!

Dr. Martin Luther King, Jr. once said: "Injustice anywhere is a threat to justice everywhere."

You see this city was a proud city as a matter of fact they actually consider themselves the first city of Asia.

They were all about position, prestige, the highest seat and the most recognition.
This city was so messed up in this arena their letter was begun by informing them that HE was the first and the last.

In other words, before the problems started I was
While the problem exists I am
When the problems are over I shall be

I am the first and the last; point blank! So stand up.

This Church was faithful to Christ though ridiculed, mocked, abused, cursed, loss of property (San Augustine property taxes raised 33 percent), imprisonment and possible martyrdom.

These folk were losing their jobs and becoming poorer and then forced out of their homes; but they held fast to their beliefs.

You see what happened was Rome passed a law of loyalty and once a year you would have to appear before officials and proclaim that Caesar is Lord. If you did not do this, you ran the risk of losing everything.

You see this church was spiritually rich but outwardly poor.

- The question we must ask ourselves is in Heaven are we viewed as the Church of the Living God or of the synagogue of satan? We professed to be of the faith but really are not!

We shall receive a crown of life. For standing up!

We will also be saved from the second death which is the lake of fire!

Doctor M. E. Lyons

He closes like every other; he that hath an ear let them hear what the spirit saith unto the church. It is the duty of the believer to hear the message.

Revelation 3: 1-6

Phonetics: Sar-dease

Sardis was had two sections: the first one sat on a ridge that originated out of the side of a mountain; fifteen hundred feet straight up. And was impregnable and no enemy could get to them.

When they outgrew this ridge, they started another place at the base and bottom of the mountain in the valley.

Record was that gold was found just floating along in the valley in the waters flowing through the city.

Their pride was built on wealth and security from their enemies.

When John wrote this, things had changed. They lived on what happened in the past and were totally ignorant of what the present day brought.

They knew about the Lord from the days of their ancestors but they were far from that now!

Sardis had only been conquered twice. When Cyrus was opposing them a guard was said to have dropped his helmet over that steep wall and climbed down to get it through the crevices; and that very night a band of soldiers came back up through the crevices they saw the guard crawl down.

Later on someone remembered this and under Alexander the Great they were defeated in the same manner.

Now understand Jesus has the seven stars in His hands; He holds the Ministers and Preachers/Pastors in His hands.

Now watch this: they have been chosen by God to do EXACTLY what they are told; regardless of what others may say!

Seven is the number of perfection which denotes that He gives His full power of the Holy Spirit to those He has sent to carry out His work.

Stars imply brilliance and glory. There should be a brilliancy of glory shown in the angel of the Church; when we are in His hands! Completely in His hands there should be no reason for the person who cannot stand the Pastor to have to admit it. (Even in their mind if they will not admit it verbally that God has him in His hands)

They were placed in a dead Church by the hand of Christ; now what does this suggest? This suggests that a Church is never complete unless there is a Man of God in the helm.

He has been placed there to first be aroused and excited himself and thereto arouses the Church.

I want you to see something real quick: He says thou hast a name that thou livest.

Name in Greek is <u>ON-ON-AH</u> which means a reputation.

- Get this; they were trying to live up to what they were known for; rather than up to what God desired.

- You know it's dangerous to try and live up to a reputation.
- You will go broke trying to do that
  a. Spiritually
  b. Emotionally
  c. Mentally
  d. Financially
  e. Politically

<u>M.E. Lyons quote: When a person tries to live up to a reputation that was incorrect from the beginning; nothing correct can come out of it!</u>

Doctor M. E. Lyons

They were known for their vitality (physical strength and mental vigor) but the heart searcher saw the real deal.

You see they were living in ruins but were so caught up on yesteryear they could not see their present state.

Wouldn't be terrible for your name to be known among many as being alive; but get to Heaven and said that you were <u>DEAD</u>?

You see the problem with Sardis was that they were complacent. This was the complaint.

- They were a dying Church
1. They had works
   a. Programs
   b. Ministries
   c. Activities

- They had a great reputation in the community; BUT DEAD!
- Others looked at them for being progressive
- Alive
- Well attended
- Well liked
- Prosperous
- Busy
- Full of works
- Right beliefs
- Doctrinally sound

Notice that in verse two it says, yet they were not ALL totally dead.

1. You see we need to let what life is around us to help the others.
   a. Although they were some living things and people; they were on their way to dying as well.
   b. What this teaches us is that if death is in the Church Spiritually we need to be careful because it will begin to work on us if we are not careful.

1. What are you saying?
   a. Busy-bodies
   b. Idle talk
   c. Lying tongues
   d. Non-progressive thinkers
   e. Past dwellers

What does it mean to die spiritually?
1. To have a form of Worship, but to deny the power thereof. (II Timothy 3:5) We must become vulnerable to the Holy Spirit.
2. To focus on ritual, traditional worship instead of Christ
   a. As long as the end result is Christ is received. (Christ cannot be received through anything that is not like Him. But if He is received it is proof that He approves!)
   b. To focus upon activities instead of Christ
   c. To become formal (being in accordance with usual requirements) in Worship instead of alive in Christ.
      1. What worked for you; may not work for me!
      2. Same Message; different Method (You have no right looking down on me for how I Worship, Sing, Preach, Pray, Praise, just because it is not the way you do it, or the way they used to do it, or not like what you are used to).
   d. To conduct activities in order to keeps the organization going instead of learning about Christ.
      1. Not to just throw things, Ministries together just to get people involved have a desired result spiritually for the Ministry.
      2. Ask different ones what is the purpose of their Ministry! Ushers, Choir, Mission. Brotherhood. (Do not just make something up; let it be sincere; would the others in your Ministry say the same thing? Are they aware of the purpose of the Ministry you are a part of or give leadership to?)
      3. To hold services and activities for social fellowship instead of spiritual growth. (Which is more important? Usually without answering it will show up in the purpose of our gatherings.)

4. To lose our zeal for witnessing for Christ and to see others grow in Christ
5. To become lethargic in the study of God's Word. We do not like to study and then when we do we do it because we have to teach or preach instead of out of Love.

- We must ask ourselves the questions on a personal note and see where we stand; perhaps we are more like Sardis than we know!!!

This Church had its lamp-stand removed for several years and now they are afforded another opportunity.

Verse 2 says: be watchful.

- This is a warning and indicator that something else is the matter.

1. The Church was doing what she was supposed to be doing!
   a. The problem was with their spirit.

1. They were not focusing upon Christ and His cause!
2. They were literally sitting in services half asleep.
3. They were allowing their thoughts to wander.
4. Instead of hungering for the Word; they were hungering after worldly things.
5. They held activities for the sake of fellowship and because it was what we are supposed to do.

- When he uses the word WATCH it suggests waking up and becoming alive!
- They needed to re-visit why it was that they were really coming to Church anyhow.
- Think about what their true calling is; not what arouses their flesh.
- Why they were placed on earth

You see the word watch is imperative; which implies that it is a command not a request!

    a. Now we need not take this too lightly; Christ commands us to do something or else kind of situation!

    b. Not only is the word watch imperative but it is in the present tense!

1. Saying that RIGHT NOW; we need to become watchers!
2. Recognize NOW
3. Rethink NOW
4. Rearrange our priorities NOW

We ought to periodically do a WATCH APPRAISAL (How far away are we from what we called and sent here to do?)

- Then He says: Strengthen the things which remain...

– Not everything that was done; was wrong.

– Give strict and immediate attention to these things! (They started out strong; but they have weakened to the point of death now!)

– Otherwise, don't just watch; DO SOMETHING!

– If it is not our Ministry we do not support it; we will watch another Ministry die; for the sake of saying; <u>MINES IS STIL LIVING</u>! The problem is; yours cannot live if mines is dying!

– Not one ministry had ever been completed or carried out like it should be-at least not in the eyes of Christ!

1. Now watch this: He uses the word perfect here!
2. PLAY-RAH-OH; which means: complete, ending, or to be full.
3. The definitions I want to zero in on is that it means to LEVEL UP and to SATISFY.

    A. He literally says Ministry is never Ministry that He is SATISFIED with until we level up. (In playing games; you cannot just skip levels...you have to beat everything on that level before you can get to the next level...our problem is that we never complete Ministry and SATISFY God until we can lay everything else down and LEVEL UP!)

1. We are so divided; our Ministry raised more money than your Ministry
2. Your Ministry does not give as much money as our Ministry.
3. Your Ministry is not as important as our Ministry.
4. My Ministry was started in this Church 115 years ago.

Christ says: He had not found their works PERFECTED before God.

– In other words, I will not go to bat for you until you make a concerted effort to make a CHANGE! (Ephesians 5:27)

He says strengthen them; <u>BECAUSE THEY ARE READY TO DIE AS WELL.</u>

Obviously: what was; is no more.

– Devotion (You were so ready to spend time with the Master)

• What is devotion?
• Ask the question…
• Devotion is our consecrating ourselves with God;
• It actually means dedicating this service to God.

(However we start is what we say is how we will finish)

1. Personal- start our day with devotion
2. Corporate Devotion- we used to rush trying to get there for devotion; that is where the fire was!
3. Lifestyle Devotion- how we live; will let everyone else know our devotion; after all the root word of devotion is devoted which a derivative is of devote.

<u>Devote means: to give up or concentrate on a particular pursuit.</u>

– Readiness and love for everybody

We treated everyone with respect and love; and then we became comfortable in our Christianity. Christianity is not comfortable! Jot this down.

1. We have to love those who use and abuse us
2. We have to witness
3. We have to work
4. We have to pray constantly (fervently)

– Service- we volunteered; and did not have to be begged to do anything.
– Witnessing- shared the Gospel with anyone we came into contact with; why not have a goal to share Christ with at least three people a day?

• We sin; when we lose our fervor and zeal to serve, praise, and worship Christ.
• How so? Anything that is not right is wrong!
• Serving God is right
• Worshipping God is right
• True devotion is right/Real Worship is right

When we lose our heat that should be in our light; we sin. Because anything that is not light; is DARKNESS! We become sinners when we lose our fervency.

Verse 3 says (Have it read aloud): If we as Christians refuse to watch (wake up), refuse to arouse ourselves; scripture says He will come to judge as a thief.

The Church will then be of no worth to the Kingdom. Wouldn't it be sad to have been in existence for One Hundred and fifteen years and it is for naught?

a. Mark 8:36
b. Matthew 7:27

I.   In the fourth verse is says that there are some in the Church who have not DEFILED which in essence means to SOIL their clothes with evil.

      a.   Defile means moo-loo-no means to blacken.
      b.   But He says they will walk with me in white. (Not because they have not soiled their clothes, but because they are not continuously soiling their clothes.)

Church at Philadelphia

18,000 inhabitants' approximately five Churches and about 3,000 Christian city goers

The city sat over a large earthquake vault.

It was said that in A.D. 17 a horrifying earthquake hit an area and it completely destroyed Sardis and ten other cities.

Philadelphia was completely spared of total destruction. For ten years the city felt tremors; each time reminding them of what had happened.

Future generations would be reminded in every shaking of what had taken place before.

- They would have to evacuate the city during these times and then verse 12 says that he shall go no more out!
- Philadelphia began to rebuild and received assistance by Tiberius and thereby changed the name of the city to Neocaesarea which is the New city of Caesar as verse 12 says.

–   The name Philadelphia means brotherly love.
–   The very name of their Church was a constant reminder that if there was no love their missionary work could not happen.
–   This Church was a missionary minded Church! Verse 8.

I.   He is speaking to the angel/Pastor

      a.   His prerequisites to the Angel:

1. He must live in the Word
2. Live on his face in prayer
3. Preach and Teach the Word of God
4. Exhort the believers to live for Christ, to study the Word, pray, witness, and Minister faithfully.
5. Lead the Church to set up the ministries that would reach the lost, build up the believers, minister to the needy, and reach out to the world by supporting worldwide missions.

- You see if the Pastor/Angel were to slack up on any of these; the Church would lose her focus on Jesus.
- She would no longer be faithful.
- This would ensure the life of the Church

Key of David that opens and no man shuts; and shuts; no man opens. Isaiah 22:22- Jesus alone determines who can get into Heaven.

- King Hezekiah had a servant named Eliakim. He was the personal secretary to Hezekiah; he was in complete control of who could gain entrance into the king. Nobody could get in without seeing Eliakim.
- No one could enter the king's court without Eliakim's permission.

II.   This Church is commended for three things:

- The Church used the open door of Evangelism (Reach the lost) and Missions (Go and assist/relieve in needed areas; a group of individuals sent to a foreign country to yield assistance). Matthew 28: 19, 20.
- This one kind of blew my mind: She was a Church strategically located: she bordered three other towns: Lydia, Mysia, and Phrygia. Perfect place for Evangelism and Missions.

    a.   Consider this: the city/Church was not placed and built in places where it was a growing community for growth; it was placed in a place where the need was the greatest.

    b.   They were more interested in being in a neighborhood that needed Christ.

    c.   More interested in building where Christian potential was the best and not where the money was/is.

    d.   They were commended for their work in these efforts.

    e.   He says I have set an open door before you and you just walked right through it.

– I put in you in a place to witness and work and you did just that.

– A door: what is a door? It is a walkway that takes you from one place to the next; it has a threshold and a threshold is to indicate that one place is behind you while another is in front of you!

– Door signifies great <u>OPPORTUNITIES</u>!

– Free and unrestrained access

– We would have power to reject anyone or accept anyone into the house. (The choice is ours: the problem is there is more rejecting than there is accepting!)

Watch this: Jesus says because you have exercised your walking through the door…NO MAN CAN SHUT IT.

1.   There will be continuous <u>TRAFFIC</u>- growth- people recognizing something is going on.

2.   Continuous <u>TESTS</u>-potential-what you can deal with and handle

3.   Continuous <u>TENDER/TREASURE</u>-gifts- finance your future. He will not open a door and not give necessary tools to carry it out if you have faith enough to walk through it.

4.   Continuous <u>TOUCH</u>- anointing- I will watch the door; no man can shut, which means my hands are upon you and your works.

• Notice also that the Church had LITTLE STRENGTH.

    a.   The Church was small in number-3x

1. We are too small to do that/this.
2. We are not able to do this/that
3. These excuses were not uttered because the door was not opened by man.

- I have set before thee an OPEN DOOR and no man can shut it.

    a. Be careful what side you are on, because the door could be shut in any of our faces and opened against our will for others.
    b. There is a COLON placed after this very bold statement.
    c. Colon indicates that which comes after the previous statement is an elaboration or implication of the whole matter.

- In other words, Jesus desires for us to know that the Church who practices this mindset is the Church that God will use for Ministry and even finance, empower, and enlighten to what needs to be done.

- How so? There is an OPEN DOOR! For all who do not rely, refer, and always reference their strength.

Now keep in mind there is reference to the Corporate Church and the Individual Churches which are us.

1. We have minimized God so much so that we do not know the God He desires for us to know; we want everything to make sense.

They were small in number and small in resources; yet they made strides all over the place to carry out the mandates and dictates of Christ.
If we would but only start trusting God more and stop trying to make sense out of spiritual things; God could do the impossible. I Corinthians 2:14

When it speaks of being Jewish; it is not speaking about outwardly of the descent it speaks of inwardly one who believes in Jesus Christ.
There were Jews in Philadelphia who were persecuting the believers. They claimed to be followers of Christ and Jews; but were not.

Reason being because love was not present.

I will make them worship at thy feet. In other words, the Gentiles or opposers will be converted; <u>IF</u> you do this my way!

Verse 10 speaks about the Great Tribulation Matthew 24:21
- Believers will be delivered from this time.
- This happens in the end times. A time that would surpass any hard time the world has ever seen.

Great tribulation will encumber two fallings upon the earth:
- The persecution by the Antichrist-Revelation 13: 7-8
- Judgment over all those who rejected Jesus Revelation 19: 1-3

Church at Laodicea
Revelation 3: 14-22

History of the Church: this was the chief city of Phrygia.

Extremely wealthy and prosperous city
It had three of the most important highways around it.
   a. It was a banking center
   b. Clothing manufacturing center
   c. Had a famous medical school known for the eye salve it produced

The issue with this Church is with their placement.
- Their commitment is in question
- Their allegiance is shaky
- Their choice is unclear.

- This is the final Church addressed by Christ and is by far the worst Church
- God does not command them to do anything because they are SET in their ways.
- He absolutely has nothing good to say of this Church.

   a. This is a Church that might as well not even exist.
   b. No good to the body AT ALL.
   c. They do not intend to do well.

Look at the characteristics of the Church mentioned:

1. Complacent
2. Lethargic
3. Self-satisfied
4. No heart/Half-Hearted- you just never knew with them
5. Neutral

It all begins with the Pastor to be either hot or cold!
Now notice something that I never had clarity on until now.

- Hot or cold- which simply suggests do not straddle the fence; be one or the other.
- Don't leave me guessing; BE FOR ME or AGAINST ME!
- It is simply shocking that Christ would basically say: "I would rather you have no commitment than just some commitment!"

I. Lukewarm person does not know they need clothing or heat.
II. Cold person does realize they need it. (Luke 18:11 KJV, The Message)

- It is a challenge to the Pastor to address those who are lukewarm! (Wow; a lot of people get angry with Pastors because he addresses those who are lukewarm!)

  a. The problem with being lukewarm is it upsets the stomach of God!
  b. Being lukewarm meant that the Church were more concerned with rituals, ceremonies and programs to be acceptable to God. (Luke 9:23-27-The Message)

- Lukewarm Churches are only half committed to spreading the Word!
- Lukewarm Churches are only have committed to teaching the Word of God.
- Lukewarm Churches are only have committed to living a pure life for Christ-(II Corinthians 6: 17, 18; Hebrews 12:14)
- Lukewarm Church is only have committed to the Church (They portray they are fully committed but actions prove half-committed)

- Lukewarm Church are only half committed to giving (I Corinthians 16:2)

Now get this: they were known for money, clothes, and optical school and salve.

Most people who attend Church attend just enough to salve (soothe) their consciences and feel acceptable to God.

Some think God would not reject them.
If you are going to be lukewarm; He would rather you not even, make no profession at all.

When a person is comfortable it is the most difficult thing to do is to make a FLAME appear in either a cold or lukewarm place.

Fire can only take place when heat is being introduced; but if cold is the cold or lukewarm is the climate; heat cannot produce fire!

- He says: "I will spew you out of my mouth!"
- This is used to create a graphic picture for us.

But right here Jesus the AMEN says you that you are POOR, NAKED, and BLIND!

Jesus describes Himself to the Church as the AMEN!

AMEN means truth.

He literally says heed my Words because I am the AMEN! (TRUTH)

Jesus is actually what the Church is not!
Revelation 4: 1-11

We are now speaking about the throne of God!

God has spoken to the Churches and listed their failures and warned them of their statuses.

He also has given them what could be theirs if change was in their future.

Now He speaks of the things that are coming to earth.

Notice that scripture never alludes that He will come but that He IS coming. Present tense!!!

The church will not be mentioned anymore as being on earth.

It is thought that the church was taken to Heaven by the end of chapter three.

Once the church has been raptured; the Lord will then begin dealing with Israel again and then Tribulation will begin.
(Seven-year period in which the Lord will deal with the Jewish people concerning their rejection of the Messiah)

They will still have a chance to accept Christ and be saved; and those who reject Christ will be destroyed.

Chapter four introduces us to the beginning of the Tribulation period.

John entering Heaven right here is where many scholars and theologs believe the church is entering Heaven.

God's reference to showing John the things that should happen after this is Tribulation; we will see these things taking place.
The throne that is spoken of is the throne of judgment.

Beasts with all of the eyes symbolized the depth of vision.
(The beast are said to be a combination of the cherubim in Ezekiel 10 and the seraphim's in Isaiah 6)

They guard the throne of God.

Listen at the description of God!

The jasper represented Reuben; Jacob's firstborn.

The sardius represented Benjamin his lastborn.

Reuben's name means behold a son, and Benjamin means so of my right hand!

So in essence to look upon God makes one consider and look at His son who is at His right hand!

"No man cometh unto the Father except by me!"

Verses 9 and 10 whenever the creatures worship God; the twenty-four elders lay prostrate before God!
Notice there are three doors in Revelation:
Door of evangelism and missions
Door of our heart
Door of revelation

Because after we have opened the door of our heart god will begin to reveal things to us.

God is described with things that are of a brilliant light.

The twenty-four elders are speculated to be the leaders in both the Old Testament and the New Testament; twelve patriarchs and twelve apostles.

- The twelve patriarch's names are on the twelve gates of the New Jerusalem and the Apostles names are on the foundations. (Revelation 21: 12, 14)

One of the beast is like a
Lion- supremacy reign
Ox- strength
Man- intelligence
Eagle- swiftness

All of them are there to glorify God.

This also shows that everything is created to glorify God. Animal and Man.

Notice what the leaders did; at the singing of the song they FELL down and worshipped God and threw their crowns before the throne and Worshipped God. This portrays that those who will not worship God in their deeds and actions will not and are not worthy of eternal life!

Revelation 5: 1-14

God is now holding a book that has seven seals binding it together which has in it the record of judgments that should fall upon the earth before the Lord can set up His kingdom.

The book is in His right hand and the picture is He is extending the book out for someone to open it.

Now understand the book is in His RIGHT hand!
Hand of power.
No mere mortal has the power to remove.

This also shows us that God holds our future in His hands. No one can control their future.
(Alister McGrath in his book Christianity's dangerous idea; says that man can bestow righteousness upon him and ultimately become saved through that measure.)

There was writing on the front and back of the book/scroll; usually written on papyrus/papyri. It is the equivalent to our 8.5 by 11 and was rolled up and a string tied around the end and it apparently was so much needed to be done it took up the front and back which never was used. Sealed seven times!

He also A strong angel puts forth an appeal for someone to open the book and break the seals. He then goes down the list.

Strong angel; strong enough to shout and the entire world hear the invitation but too weak to open the book!

Made the request in the
Celestial
Terrestrial
Subterranean

No one could do it.

No angel man or demon.

John was thinking that everything that was done on earth would not be corrected. Now the wicked would go unpunished.

David did say the ungodly are not so.
He then said it was not until he went until the sanctuary that he saw the end of the wicked and now nobody can open the book!

John began to cry. And one of the elders consoled him and said don't cry; there is one who can; you just did not recognize him.

Lion of Judah
Root of David was qualified to open the book

Notice that in Revelation Jesus is referred to as a Lamb and a Lion!
As the Lamb He is the sacrificial one.
As the Lion He is the judge, punishing His enemies.

- At His first coming He came as the Lamb
- When He comes again he is coming as the Lion.

You see when John saw the Lamb who was just referred to as a Lion He looked as if He had just been slain!

So we will be able to see His nail scarred hands/feet and side in Heaven.

Understand this to John he saw a Lamb; but to everyone else they saw a Lion.

He was Lamb to John because he was about to lose hope but to those He was headed to see they would see the Lion because of their wrongdoings and non-repentance.
He had seven horns- symbolized omnipotence (all power; cannot get away)
He had seven eyes- symbolized omniscience (all wise, to know everything)

When Jesus took the book out of the right hand of God the beasts and elders went to worshipping the Lamb.

They each had a harp for their song and a vial or bowl of incense.

The bowl of incense was a collection of EVERY prayer ever prayed!

Prayers were being answered even at the hour. After you have left off of the scene.

Then there was the choir of millions perhaps billions who were singing; heavenly choir-

In closing this book is official document of the last days of human history.

Revelation 6

> ➤ Now the drama begins
> ➤ The Book's content is about to be revealed (Notice the seals are merely being broken not the book opened)
> ➤ Four horsemen are about to be released

A. The Lamb opens the first seal and there is a white horse and a rider with a bow in his hand.

- Some say this is Jesus riding on the WHITE HORSE others say it is the anti-Christ (personal opponent of Christ; one who will spread evil throughout the earth before being conquered at Christ's second coming)! Matthew 24:5

- Christ does not possess a bow; weapons of war are not a part of who He is!
- This rider is given a crown; Christ wore a crown throughout all of his life on earth; He is the King of Kings.
- The rider wishes to go out and conquer; Christ's mission is for salvation.
- The record is the anti-Christ seeks to conquer through deception; which means that he looks like him and has the appearance but is not HIM. (In movies they have a double for the President so that if something happens to one the true one is still alive). (Impersonators look like the original but cannot be them)

The record said he went forth conquering.

1. Some scholars say this is evidence of the cold war to come.
2. Other say this could be a missile attack; because an arrow is a weapon of distance, but the rider does not initiate war here in this verse.
3. Peace is not taken from earth until the second seal.

B. <u>The second living creature calls and summons John over and the second rider comes forth with a great sword on a fire red horse.</u>

1. Hand to hand combat is implied.
2. This is where peace is removed from the earth.

- ❖ This rider will cause those who are waiting on earth to divide themselves.
- ❖ Race against race
- ❖ Class against class
- ❖ Neighbor against neighbor
- ❖ Employee against employee
- ❖ Husband against wife
- ❖ Religion against religion
- ❖ Nation against nation

The last days will be wars and rumors of wars; is hinted at right here. Matthew 24: 6, 7

   3. This rider removes peace in earth.
   4. Cause as much division as he came and ruins every type of relationship
      a. Who is the rider; we do not know for certain; but Revelation 12:3

   C. This rider comes forth holding scales on a black horse.

   1. This represents famine in the land; which most times follows a war.
   2. The voice that comes out speaks about the scales; which are used as weights to grain that was being rationed during a famine.
   3. This rider seems to control the economy

   i. A penny is what is called a denarius and could buy a measure of wheat; about a quart
   ii. A penny to buy three measures of barley/wheat
   iii. Penny was a day's wage. (Imagine working all day and having enough just to eat; no home, nothing else.) No extra for family.

   D. Then comes a pale (ashy; black and blue in color) horse with death and Hades as its riders.

   1. Here there is implication that whatever is no scared to death by the arrow; and those who are not killed by the sword, and those who will not starve to death, death and hell will get them.
   2. Death by genocide (death of a nation) such as Hitler with Holocaust or Stalin with Siberia where millions were killed, and others.

III.   Scripture now speaks of the martyrs of the tribulation period!

   a. Matthew 24:9
   b. Those who are faithful unto death there is a special place in Heaven near and dear to Him; in His throne under the altar! Matthew 16:25

    c. Those who go out and Preach the Gospel and are slain are the ones under the altar!

    d. They cry out to God to avenge their blood. Verse 6

    e. White robes are then given to the martyrs; a symbol of righteousness.

E. <u>The sixth seal is now opened.</u>

1. This seal causes nature to go into convulsions

    a. Great earthquake shakes the land and the sea

    b. The starry heavens go into disarray

    c. The sun's light bulb goes out

    d. The moon begins to ooze blood

    e. Stars drop as figs when ripened (meteor shower heavenly fireworks)

    f. The sky retracted as a scroll being rolled up

    g. Mountains and hills started jumping up and down in panic mode

    h. The people ran to the mountains/and rocks to hide their faces

o <u>This ought to sound familiar; when Jesus died…</u>

o The seventh seal has not yet been opened; so the book cannot be read yet!

Revelation 7

— Chapter six ends asking the question; who will be able to stand and chapter seven opens up with the answer.

• This book now held in the hands of God is what is to take place at the end of the world.

1. The book is so secretive and important that it is bound by seven seals.

2. God gives us a glimpse into the end times.

3. He does this to warn us to turn to His Son!

4. In order to avoid this judgment, we must become true followers of Christ.

5. Six seals are broken by now.

6. This is just the beginning with the four horsemen and other happenings.

7. The seventh seal will mark that the great tribulation.

I. There is a remnant that is saved here: 144,000

~ <u>Out of all the tribes that normally are listed in the Old Testament of the twelve tribes Ephraim (Hebrew name is Manasseh) and Dan are missing.</u>

~ <u>Joseph and Benjamin are listed in Revelation but not in Genesis 49; read it and it lists all of the sons and tribes of Jacob.</u>

~ They may have been omitted because they were leaders in idolatry.

a. The winds of God's judgment are in His hands and the hands of the four angels.

b. They are not in the hands of an evil force; but Gods hands.

c. He delays the judgment

II. Four corners of the earth:

1. North, South, East, and West
   a. In other words, a great storm is about to be loosed on the earth.

2. This covers every inch of the earth.

3. He is buying time to seal all of the servants of God. (Even before they know and they are servants of God)
   a. He knows who will be saved and who will not and gives them ample time to change.
   b. Seal means a mark of possession, power, preservation, and protection.
   c. He seals them to notify the antichrist the beast to leave them alone.
   d. The SEAL and the MARK.

e.   Some folk think that the antichrist will come from the tribe of Dan-Genesis 49:17

f.   God will judge those who are followers of the antichrist. (hand out)

4.   The believers will not suffer the judgment of God; but they will suffer the 3 ½ year's persecution and slaughter of the antichrist Revelation 7:14.

a.   Israel will be saved in the end times; we are Israel.

b.   This is who will be saved in the end times and from where.

c.   These are virgins Revelations 14: 4,5

d.   The worst holocaust the world has ever seen will take place at this time.

Verse nine means they will be holding PALM branches; which symbolizes victory! (As it were when Jesus rode into to town!) They laid down victory but victimized Jesus)

Angels sing but they can never sing of salvation and know what it feels to be saved so their song is woefully limited.

Revelation 8

-   This is the opening of the seventh seal!

1.   In the event of opening the seventh seal and the silence; seven angels leap from the pages of the book and take their places with the issuance of the seven trumpets.

-   They was a moment of silence in Heaven for what was about to take place.

1.   It had them in awe; Jesus did not move or speak and Heaven was at a standstill concerning what was about to happen.

-   These trumpets will affect our ecological system because trumpets always signify God's interference in human history.

1. <u>A trumpet does three things.</u>
   a. Waken form a slumber or sleep
   b. Announce Royalty
   c. Announce war

I. The angel who offers the incense is none other than Jesus because he offers incense. (What is incense used for; to freshen a smell that is unbecoming.)

   — Much incense the Bible reads.
   — This is a priestly role of Christ and Him making intercession for us again.
   — These are prayers of those who are in earth during the great tribulation.
   — Jesus actually adds power and fragrance to the prayers of those in the Church

   • The trumpets begin to sound and a third of the earth is destroyed.
   • They are blown o yield a warning of the judgment to come.
   • The first four trumpets being blown represent the parts of life which men take for granted.

1. <u>Land, sea, fresh water, and heavenly bodies</u>

   — The first trumpet affects vegetation and it evidently causes no vegetation to grow; which in turn causes a FAMINE!

1. <u>First a fierce storm like none other; Katrina is a baby compared to this.</u>

   a. It will rain hail that looks like fire mingled with blood.
   b. The winds will be so strong it is carried across a third of the earth! WOW.

2. <u>The trees, and green grass is gone; if the green grass is gone that means there will be no brown grass; if the brown grass is gone</u>

there will be no food for the animals; if there will be no food for the animals; there will be no food for us.

3. Bring back any memories of anything; the horse to bring about famine; the third horsemen- Rev. 6: 5-6!

— Second trumpet indicates a massive volcanic eruption.

• The explosion will eject a rock so massive it appears to be a mountain and when it hits the earth water it is covered in blood and cause what it hits to be in blood.

1. A mountain is representative of a kingdom and fire represents judgment in most cases.
   a. So in essence every kingdom still standing will be judged by the blowing of this trumpet.
   b. Jeremiah 51: 25, 42 explains the prophecy most likely to have been the fall of Babylon.
   c. This can be any city whose mindset that they could not be defeated.

— The third trumpet verses 10-11 speaks about ships being upon the water in depth.

   a. Meteoric mass
   b. Remember that stars normally represent ANGELS.
   c. BUT the angel is falling which says to us the fall of a people under the judgment of God.
   d. Wormwood is the name and is toxic if ingested over a period of time. Jeremiah 9:15
   e. Pollution in the water and fresh water supplies would be no more.
   f. THINK ABOUT THIS: what do you bathe in: WATER
   g. What do we drink; WATER
   h. What is everything made from predominantly; WATER?
   i. Some way or another everything is tied to water!

1. You will either drink poisonous water or die from thirst!
2. Notice it was a GREAT STAR! (Degree of punishment) Jeremiah 2:13

2. When men prefer the bitter waters of idolatry over the sweet waters from the living fountain; they will receive these bitter waters with the fatal consequences that follow!

– Implies that no ships will sail and no one will work the waters which in turn suggests that no there will also be no commerce. Verse 9

   a. 1/3 part of creatures in the sea
   b. 1/3 part of the ships
   c. There will be human life on the ships; so they will not make it.
   d. Notice that we do not know if this will be the same 1/3 of the earth it could all be different 1/3 of the earth which if added up covers the whole earth.

1. No shipments; there will be no way of trading and shipping and receiving any goods from anywhere.
2. Understand that the stars are issuing warnings not the actual blow.

– The fourth trumpet cause a third of everything to be blacked out.

1. Astronomical eclipse
2. 1/3 of the sun- day will seem as night
3. 1/3 of the moon- night life will be more difficult
4. 1/3 of the stars- we normally look to stars for direction (Whether you know it or not-directions are based off of stars)

• Then there was an angel for the most part; firing off sounding shots and warning shots to those who are in the earth. Woe, woe, woe; if you think this is bad wait for the last three!

REVELATION 9

- These last three trumpets are called the <u>WOE trumpets</u>.

- Notice when the star is referred to John uses a personal pronoun and says: HIM!
- It is said that he was a star; because it says; fallen; in past tense and was given the keys!
- Fallen star may be an angel or satan himself. (Luke 10:18)
- Isaiah 14: 12-15
- He had the key to the bottomless pit-the abyss
- Billows of smoke poured out as it were from a furnace
- Jesus allows satan or the fallen star to wreak havoc on the evil these men have done to reap what they have sown!

    a. So is the implication here; those who continue to do their evil and will not change be a part of this company; YES!

    b. The men and women who have sown so much evil and do not seriously have the seal will be in this number! Galatians- <u>REAP-SOW</u>

    c. The seal can only be those who do as the Churches were heeded; hear what the spirit saith unto the Churches! Then you are sealed!!!

    d. The seal happens during the great tribulation (Revelation 7: 2, 3)

1. Swarms of locusts came forth from the smoke
2. Their power was somewhat restricted
3. Locusts are also a symbol of God's anger upon the ungodly

    a. Locusts normally devour every green thing; but are withheld this time now they sought out to preserve them!

    b. Locusts are a symbol of destruction.

    c. They are advised to seek out men without the seal.

    d. The sting was not fatal; but tormenting

    e. The sting was so bad it caused men to want to die

    f. It happens repeatedly

g. They will desire to die but cannot

h. They will look for death and death will escape them (It is as if they had a loaded gun and put it to their heads and it shot them in the brain but they did not die; tried it again damaged but did not kill them.)

i. They will crave death. Jeremiah 8:3

Appearance of the locusts:

1. Crowns like gold-authorization to rule in men's lives
2. Faces of men-creatures of intelligence
3. Hair as women- attractive and seductive; to seem innocent and harmless
4. Teeth as lions-they were ferocious and cruel
5. Breastplates of iron-difficult to attack and destroy
6. Sound of wings-like rushing too battle-terrifying and demoralizing
7. Tails as scorpions- equipped them torment both mentally and physically
8. Like horses-conquering host
9. Five months-unrelieved suffering

• They had a king; which in Hebrew means: Abaddon (destruction) but in Greek is: Apollyon (destroyer) a reference to satan.

– The say that one day here represents a year...so 150 years.

This would make 365 1-4, plus 30, plus 1, plus 1-12, equal 396 1-3 days. Or, a day being a symbol of a year, three hundred and ninety-six years and four months.

God has already set the date and time for judgment; WE JUST DO NOT KNOW WHEN!

Sixth trumpet sounds:

1. Four angels who have been bound are now loosed to kill a third of mankind.

161

(The question is raised; are these the same four angels found in chapter 7:1?)

2. Two Hundred million riders on horses with breastplates

    a. <u>The colors of their breastplate is red</u> (fire) <u>blue</u> (hyacinth) <u>and yellow</u> (brimstone).

    b. <u>Two hundred; thousand; thousand...which is 200,000 plus the additional, 000.</u>

    c. The fire, smoke, and brimstone represents the three plagues that kill a third of mankind.

    d. Not only do these horses kill with their mouths but they wound with their tails!

    e. 2/3 of men survived this onslaught and plagues but they did not repent. WOW!

    f. Did you catch these will be able to blow fire form their mouths?

– You'll have to watch out for their heads, mouths, and tails

1. Head- intelligence
2. Mouth-deception
3. Tails- continuous destruction- POISONOUS STRIKES and DEADLY WOUNDS!
4. 2/3 survives not because they deserve it but because God is merciful

    g. Notice where this happens; the Euphrates.

1. The Euphrates River is where the first sin took place.
2. This river flowed out of the Garden of Eden. (Genesis 2:14)
3. The first murder took place. (The western boundary of the land God promised to Abraham)
4. <u>One of the sins and acts that is mentioned is sorceries; Greek PHARMAKON which we derive our word of pharmacy; a place that handles drugs.</u>
5. It actually talks about people who use drugs to control others!
6. It also includes:
    a. Astrology
    b. Palm reading

    c. Séances

    d. Fortune telling

    e. Crystal balls

    f. Other forms of witchcraft; yes, drugs are a form of witchcraft

– They also say an increase in immorality.

1. Immorality in Greek means: porneias- all forms of immorality

    a. Premarital sex

    b. Adultery

    c. Abnormal sex

    d. Animals and all sorts

- There will be an increase in thefts

1. Theft means: klemmaton- cheat and steal

Revelation 10

Came down from Heaven- the message was straight from the throne of God.

Clothed with a cloud- symbolizes majestic and glory. (The Heavens are clothed with his majesty)

Rainbow on his head- sign of mercy (Noah was shown this sign for a display of mercy Genesis 9: 12, 13)

Face that shone as the sun- light brilliance, and splendor. (Represent his holiness and purity)

Feet like pillars of fire- righteousness and strength as a messenger

He held a little book- contents unknown

Seven thundering's- number of completion and fulfillment.

But a voice form Heaven STOPS John from revealing the message from the thunders.

The voice said seal up whatever it was that the thunders said!

1. The point is that a great announcement is to be made on earth and is sent by the mightiest of messengers.
2. The power of this messenger proves that the announcement is to be heard by all.

    a. Pay close attention to importance of this announcement

- Comes straight form the throne of God
- Message of mercy
- Message of light
- Message of holiness
- Message that involves the whole universe (one foot on land and one on sea) He is so mighty that he straddles the whole earth
- Message of completeness

- The angel takes an oath; he swore with his hand lifted up...

I.

Chapter Eleven

- This is perhaps one of the most exciting and interesting chapters in Revelation.

1. John is told to take a rod and measure the Temple.
2. Measure the people who worship there
3. Measure the altar

- The words measure and rod are used in a couple of ways throughout the Bible

a. Rod can be used to measure a building for construction or restoration

b. Rod can be used to measure a place for preservation or protection

God is saying He desires for the true Worshippers of Israel preserved and protected while the antichrist conquers Jerusalem.

- Rod can also mean something to use for correction. (Shepherd's Psalm)
- What is being assessed here is that God wants the Temple and the occupants of the Temple measured for judgment and correction for everything they have done.

• In order to completely understand which meaning is to be taken into consideration we must understand that scripture says that the Antichrist will walk into the Temple and demand that those in the Temple give their allegiance to him. <u>Matthew 24:15 is tied to Daniel 9:24-27</u>

• Jesus actually said that the Antichrist would stand in the Church (The Holy Place) of the Jews in Jerusalem; you must understand that Jerusalem is looked upon as one of the most spiritual and religious places in the world. He is standing in a very sacred place!

• This is the best place to begin the revolution in the most religious place.

- The Temple was divided into four courts and they all surrounded a central building which was called the Most Holy Place or the Holy of Holies

- The courts moving outward away from the Holy place were:

1. The court of the holy place
2. The court of Israel
3. The area of Gentiles

These were the inner courts

This was a worship place for Jews only not Gentiles.

There was an outer court that was very large and designated for the Gentiles. (The court of the Gentiles)

The antichrist will already have secured the Gentiles and the proselytized; there will be no need to enter and make proclamation in their courts.

In the book of Daniel, he uses words that equal to a certain length.
   a.   Time= 1 year
   b.   Times= 2 years
   c.   Half time= ½ year

3 ½ years satan will wreak the worst havoc the world has ever known.

This will be the worst holocaust ever not just upon the Jews but: Muslims, Hindus, and any other who have strong beliefs.

II.   Two Witnesses

   1.   These are God's witnesses!
   2.   They are sent for 3 ½ years. Which means they are only used for this great tribulation period.
   3.   <u>They are condemning sin.</u>

      a.   Notice their dress; SACKCLOTH (mourning) the garb the prophets of old wore!
      b.   This signifies that the message the proclaim will not pull any punches
      c.   They are then assassinated in the city where the Lord was crucified. (Ironically we have just celebrated the death, burial and resurrection of our Savior).
      d.   The Greek actually reads THEIR LORD!
      e.   When it refers to the two witnesses as two olive trees (Spirit of God) and two candlesticks (Beacons of light) especially

in a day of such darkness; it references two Old Testament witnesses: Joshua and Zerubbabel. <u>Zechariah chapter four</u>

 f. Priest (Joshua) and Prince (Zerubbabel) and help to rebuild the Temple.

 g. Some think and thought that the two witnesses were Enoch; because he walked with God and was nought and Elijah because he was carried away in a chariot and these two had not died.

 h. Others think Moses and Elijah because of the plagues and drought.

1. Matthew 11: 13, 14
2. <u>These witnesses must be human and not merely ideas or entities they have mouths they have seen and they have heard and John said he saw their bodies in the streets.</u>

 i. We have heard many times that Jesus was the only one who died and was raised never to die again; not so these two witnesses are not found in scripture to ever died again after being resurrected by God himself!

 j. God is making their witness shine forth as a candlestick.

1. There are a few ideas that are being cast out for our consideration.
2. Ministers of God who have done a great job for the Temple should never be forgotten.
3. God calls and commissions, and empowers the Minister to Preach the Gospel
4. God raises up Ministers for certain periods of time for certain purposes; not all are raised for the same purpose.
5. He is sent to Preach on sin and corruption
6. God supplies the Minister! (Jeremiah speaks of this)

 k. The two witnesses possess great power! Just like Moses and Elijah

 l. Notice where the fire emits from!

    m. This speaks about the power in their Preaching. They have so much power and influence of God that the antichrist hesitates in killing them.

    n. They will control nature; they could cause it to rain or not to rain as did Elijah.

    o. God always gives the Preacher the power needed to complete the task. Acts 1:8

    p. How powerful is the antichrist to murder another leader and leave their bodies in the streets for three and a half days!

    q. The city is referred to as Sodom and Egypt; Sodom a place of worldliness, immorality and shameful sin and Egypt a place that enslaved and killed God's people.

    r. After their testimony the beast form the bottomless pit emerges and kills them.

1. The people started rejoicing; because the prophets that most people love the most are dead ones!
2. Their Sermons and Prophecies have been seemingly silenced.

    s. They are resurrected out of the streets before the eyes of the people in the streets.

    t. Earthquake will take out 1/10 of the city and will kill seven thousand people; and those left began praising God.

1. I am not sure where their praise will take them but they are of a changed mind.
They give worship but it is ingenuine worship they are just acknowledging the power of God not the all sufficiency of God.
2. It is a begrudgingly given worship just admitting He has power.

Chapter 12 (verses 1-5)

- This chapter actually reveals the struggle between sin and right. The conflict that is taking place in this world.
- In the last days it will be more intense than ever before.

Three things need to be considered:

1. The first character: a woman with Child-Israel verses 1 and 2
    a. Notice that the woman just appears on scene and is in Heaven.
    b. This means in some way that she is a heavenly representative of some earthly people.
    c. She is clothed with the sun and the moon under her feet, she has a crown upon her head a crown of stars; this sounds somewhat like the dream Joseph had in Genesis 37: 9-11.

-   Jacob understood exactly what Joseph meant: the sun represented Jacob
-   The moon represented his mother
-   The stars were his brothers
-   Joseph dreamed that Israel would be saved from destruction through him

    d. She is pregnant; understand what it says about the child. Revelation 12:5

-   Jesus was born to rule all nations; Psalms 2:9

-   Who is this woman?
-   Some say it is Mary;
-   Some say this is the church in general; the church did not give birth to Jesus. He gave birth to the church.

2. The second character: a great red dragon-satan verses 3 and 4

    a. Most people see the devil as a man with horns a long pointed tail while holding a pitch fork; but the truth is this is not a description of HOW he looks but rather the work he does.
    b. Satan is the highest and most glorious being ever created by God.

-   Listen to what the scripture says: he has seven heads; seven is the number of completeness and fullness

a. He is complete and has intelligence and knowledge, omniscient.

— Seven crowns- this symbolizes authority, rule, and dominion. He has a kingdom that he rules over.

— He has ten horns-great power, power that pierces, rips and tears up.

— His tail disturbs and knocks down a third of stars in HEAVEN. (The words DID CAST THEM suggest that it is past tense)

a. Which means he took a third more of angels from Heaven with him.
b. Satan is ruler of a third of Heaven.
c. Eons ago before man was ever born; satan was leader in Heaven
d. Lucifer his name means star of the morning.
e. He was the very ANOINTED CHERUB who was responsible for the very throne of God itself.
f. He was put in charge of the glory of God's throne. Isaiah 14: 12-15
g. Satan's aim is to destroy this child in the woman (Israel).
h. His design since eviction from Heaven has always been to destroy the seed of man.

— (He attacks men)
— Women are the tool; but men are the target!
— Beginning of time.
— If he can attack the seed, he can kill the seed; he will control the success of man.
— I Kings 16:11

6. He sought out and killed the house of BAA-SHAW and the record is he did not leave one who pisseth against the wall (In other words any person who stands up to piss!)
7. The enemy seeks to cause division between God and us and cause death.
8. The woman has the carrier or womb but without the SEED there cannot be woman or man!

The Seed or Line through Whom the Promised Seed Was to Come or God's Great Deliverance — The Strategies of satan to Destroy or Devour the Child and God's Great Deliverance

The Seed or Line through Whom the Promised Seed Was to Come or God's Great Deliverance	The Strategies of satan to Destroy or Devour the Child and God's Great Deliverance
→Abel's son, Adam's Son	→satan led Cain to kill Abel, but God gave Adan another son; Seth
→The early line of the godly seed	→satan led the godly line to mix with the ungodly and God had to destroy the earth and raise up Noah Genesis 6:5
→The line of Abraham, Isaac, and Jacob	→satan led Esau to threaten to kill his brother Jacob. God protected Jacob. Genesis 27:41
→The Line of David	→satan led Pharaoh to kill all male babies in Israel but God saved Moses. Exodus 1:8
→Line of sons of David	→satan led to Jehoram, one of Jehosophat sons, to kill all the sons but one-Ahaziah 2 Kings 8:25
→The Line of Ahaziah	→satan led Jehu to kill Ahaziah, and the queen's mother. Athaliah, took over the throne and killed all the sons, but God led the wife of the high priest to save one small baby, Joash. The promised seed rested in saving this baby's life. 2 Kings 9:11
→The Line of the Chosen People	→satan led King Ahassuerus to exterminate all of God's people. God gave him a restless and frightening night of sleep. The King spared the line. Esther

→The Line of the Promised Seed, Jesus himself, at His birth	→satan led King Herod to slay all babies in Bethlehem in an attempt to kill the promised child. God warned Joseph and told him to flee. Matthew 2:1
→There was the line of the Promised Seed, Jesus Himself, at His temptation	→satan tempted Jesus to jump off of cliff, Jesus chose God's way of the cross. Matthew 4:1
→The line of the Promised Seed, Jesus Himself, at His hometown, Nazareth	→Satan led the citizens of Nazareth to try and cast Jesus off of the brow of the cliff, but Jesus escaped. Luke 4:29
→The line of the Promised Seed, Jesus Himself, in facing His religionists	→satan led the religionists to hate Jesus and plot His death time and time again. John 7:1
→The line of the Promised See, Jesus Himself, on the cross	→satan led the world to put Jesus on the cross and to kill Him. But God raised Him form the dead. John 19:1

- This is how satan attempts to hurt God; by attacking the seed!
- This is why there is still war; YES, even in HEAVEN!

3. The main character: a man Child-Jesus Christ verse 5

Verses 6-17

- The curtain of Heaven is literally drawn back as we watch the unfolding of the greatest war!
- Ungodliness is challenging godliness.
- The dragon is out to destroy the heart of God.
- He accomplishes this to a certain extent by having others turn FROM God and to him.
- This attack is against the woman (Israel).

1. Verse 6 the woman flees for her life
   a. 1, 260-3 ½ years
   b. Israel will be tormented by the dragon
   c. They will be running to the hills and other places for safety.

2. War in Heaven 7-9
   a. This is really over the battle for souls in Heaven or in Hell.
   b. What an honor it is for Heaven to put up a fight for souls in Heaven.
   c. Notice the war is going on in a spiritual place!!! (Ephesians 6:12)
   d. There are actually ranks and orders of angels in Heaven.

   – Michael is an Archangel who serves God and who is over the rest of the angels. Daniel 10:21
   – He is also the guardian angel of God's people. Daniel 12:1
   – God's heart will be cut because there will be those who will never be saved and testimonies can never manifest.
   – Satan does lose the battle though.
   – This will be the final battle between evil and good!

   e. Now keep in mind while the war in Heaven is going on there is tormenting going on earth!

Let's evaluate this character we call satan!

1. He is the god of this world who blinds men's minds. II Corinthians 4:4.
2. He is the prince of this world. John 12:31
3. He is the adversary. I Chronicles 21:1
4. He is the slanderer. Matthew 4:1
5. He is the deceiver of the whole world. II Corinthians 11:3
6. He is the tempter. Matthew 4:3
7. He is the evil one. Matthew 6:13
8. He is the father of lies. John 8:44
9. He accuses the brethren. Revelation 12:10
10. He is a murderer. John 8:44

11. He is called Beelzebub. Matthew 12:24
12. He is called Belial. II Corinthians 6:15
13. He is called Abaddon. Revelation 9:11
14. He is called angel of the bottomless pit. Revelation 9:11
15. He is called Apollyon. Revelation 9:11
16. He is the enemy. Matthew 13:39
17. He is called the gates of hell. Matthew 16:18
18. He is called the great red dragon. Revelation 12:3
19. He is called a lying spirit. I Kings 22:22
20. He is called the old serpent. Revelation 12:9
21. He is called the power of darkness. Colossians 1:13
22. He is called the prince of the devils. Matthew 12:24
23. He is called the ruler of the darkness of this world. Ephesians 6:12
24. He is called the spirit that works in the children of disobedience. Ephesians 2:2
25. He is called the unclean spirit. Matthew 12:43
26. He is called the wicked one. Matthew 13:19

3. Victory and salvation won 10-11
4. The warning to earth is given 12
5. The dragon launches an attack upon the woman after birth 13-17

- Verses 13-18

— Fire to come down from Heaven; the same miracle that Elijah performed.

1. He makes it appear as if he did it; but the power is borrowed.
2. II Thessalonians 2:9
3. Luke 9:54
4. When the scripture says: in the sight of men it suggests that the entire purpose of the fire was to serve as ostentation (to impress).
5. Like many false prophets today do; there is ostentatious leaders who have many stage their handicaps, issues to wow you into becoming a follower and supporter.

6. We live in a world of pyro-techniques and big lights and mass productions to overwhelm the spirit with the flesh in its presentation that God is nowhere in this; instead of Worship there is performances.

   a. <u>Miracle crusades- God will not always heal; sometimes there has to be sustainment endued.</u>
   b. <u>Prophecies- they cannot be produced; they can only be received!</u>
   c. <u>Financial finagling- guilt giving, scared into sowing, we must only say what God says and not force the text to fit what we desire.</u>
   d. <u>How can we say we follow God; but will not follow the leader God has placed in our midst? Well, we are in the book of Revelation and it begins reiterating and being redundant for the Church to HEAR WHAT THE SPIRIT SAITH UNTO THE CHURCH!</u>

- NEVERTHELESS, we follow at our convenience
- We follow until we cannot see down the road in the physical.
- Listen to John again; he says these false prophets did these things in the SIGHT OF THE MEN!
- In other words, as long as the false prophets were in their sight their whole GOAL was to IMPRESS them. Not to impress upon them, not to live before them, not to lead by example but to do something that caused them to let their guards down and follow them without question!
- They do not have long in chapter 11 they only have 3 ½ years to do this all.

- This is the done to garner the support of those to believe. The record says that they were amazed by these acts.

- Notice the ANTI-CHRIST was wounded and was healed and was still alive. (Tried to even mimic resurrection and made a mockery of it because he never died from his wounds.)

175

- Verse 14 says he deceiveth those on earth! (not water but fire next time)
- He speaks; it will appear that his made god is God.
- They will be given the mark.

1. There is only one other mention of the word mark in the New Testament and that is in Acts 17:29-Graven.
2. As a slave in case they would leave; there place of origin is easily visible.
3. You will not be able to buy nor sell without the mark.
4. They would control the traffic in the world.
5. The person who controls traffic and commerce controls the world.
6. Man's number is 6 because he was incomplete until God brought about seven in our lives.
7. The economy will be controlled by these beasts; and it will be based upon the MARK! (Illuminati). Latin language on currency
8. Illuminati is plural of Latin; ILLUMINATUS meaning enlightened.
9. Drew membership from Masonic lodges, sworn secrecy and pledged obedience to their leaders.
10. It has been decreed in the Roman Catholic community that anyone who is not loyal to the POPE should not be patronized.

- He desires those who are of the same mindset to be marked due to association. Symbolical of allegiance.
- The mark is actually the name of the beast; in Gematria is numbers that represents a name and meaning! The meaning has yet to be found holistically.
- Verse 18 is speaking about the study of Gematria.
- Catholicism is based on Latin; Latin is the tongue that their sacred books are written in.
- The Romish Church is officially called the Latin Church; when the Church convenes and they have conferences it is conducted in the Latin tongue.
- The ancient Latin capital is where we find our name Lateinos.

- It has been stated that John's disciple Polycarp says that this beast contained the Greek letters (<u>LATEINOS</u>) <u>L-thirty, A-one, T-three, hundred, E-five, I-ten, N-fifty, O-seventy, S-two hundred.</u>
- Alphabet and numbers in Greek and Hebrew are synonymous Greek- Alpha, Beta, Delta, Gamma; Hebrew- Alef, Bet, Gimil, Daleth; is 1,2,3,4.
- 7 is the number of completion, 7 days of the week on the eighth day it is a new week; 7 notes to the scale the eighth note is a new scale.
- Jesus' name totals 888 in Greek. Every name of Jesus Biblically is divisible by eight.
- Total up all the names of satan it is divisible by thirteen (12 number of government and 13 number of satan).
- The Hebrew letters of BALAAM amount to 666 as well.

Revelation 14: 1-5

- The Lamb has now left the throne and now is in the midst of Sion.
- Antichrist will move the world toward economic prosperity, toward jobs and all.
- He will propose programs for the hungry, homeless, and diseased that will work to some degree.
- He will have some solutions for the issues of drugs, alcoholism, and problems in our society.
- A program for natural cataclysmic happenings.

Then everything begins to fall apart after dependency has been accomplished.

We can only handle so much bad news so chapter fourteen serves as hope; it serves as a picture of <u>HOPE</u>! That is the theme of this chapter!

- The first thing John sees are the believers with Jesus (The Lamb)
- Notice where the Lamb is standing; Sion: Sion is another name for Jerusalem. (Sion refers to heaven itself).
- Now look closer and see who it is that is with Him. 144,000.

- These are they who have taken a vow to stand up for Christ. John 12:26

1. Serve in John 12:26- means de-ah-kuh-neh-oh…which means to minister, to be an attendant, wait upon, one of the definitions says to act as a Christian deacon; the office of a deacon.
2. Let him imitate me. Bear what I bear. Love who/what I love. To run errands.
3. Technically a deacon or deaconess.

- Many rivers: When we hear the voice of God it will be both comforting and powerful.

- Thunder- it will call us to attention.

- The makeup of the 144,000 is that they will be virgins.

   a. They will never marry.
   b. These are not physical virgins but spiritual virgins who have received new life and has not become whorish in their serving God.
   c. They made a vow to serve God and God alone.
   d. This portion is all about commitment.
   e. After all He is alluding to us being servants

      1. We are more concerned about being served than serving
      2. We look to get more than give.
      3. We are tied up in not helping and serving because of selfish ambitions. Luke 9:23; DENY means to abstain or disown.

4. Another writer says DENY means OFF. TURN IT OFF; SELF!
5. I John 2:6- the word walk transliterates to our word of proof; which suggests that our life ought to be proof of who we are following…. not our words, but our walk!

Revelation 14: 6-19

Revelation 15

The seventh trumpet is being blown now and chapter fifteen goes into descriptive detail as to what transpires.

Gematria is certainly at work here: SEVEN

There are seven dispensations
Seven mentions of the book of life
Revelation is a book of sevens
Seven Churches
Seven seals
Seven trumpets
Seven personages
Seven vials
Seven blows of the trumpets

It completes it all

When asked how many times to forgive our brother it was said; seven times seventy.
Otherwise keep forgiving until you are complete.

Israel was in captivity seventy years

Life operates in seven; changes in our bodies take place every seven years.

Seven bones in our neck
Seven bones on our face
Seven bones in our ankle
Seven holes in our head

Physiology is built around the law of seven

Fevers and gout normally last seven, fourteen, or twenty-one days. Those are the critical days

If you notice something as small as a snowflake it has seven edges when it crystallizes

Seven means complete whenever you read it in the Bible

This is where human history ends on this earth.

No more can he endure:

Backbiting
Jealousy
Rebellion
Cursing
Immorality
Thievery
Murder
Lasciviousness

Now keep in mind that this tribulatory period will last seven years.

It will be separated into two periods.

1. 1st period will be 3 ½ years and it is labeled as the <u>Beginning of Sorrows.</u>
2. The second period will be 3 ½ years and called the <u>Great Tribulation.</u>

- During the tribulation period the first 3 ½ years will have seven seal judgments that take place on the earth Revelation 6:1-7:17
- When the Great Tribulation begins the last 3 ½ years will encounter seven trumpet judgments that will take place on the earth Revelation 8:1-14:20.
- Then at the end of the period of tribulation there will be seven more judgments, seven bowl judgments and they will end human history as we know it.

- Judgment is to begin in Heaven

    –   The sign is great and marvelous

1. It is awesome to incite those who are watching to notice the awesomeness of God

    –   A sign of seven mighty angels prepared to go before God

1. <u>Believers will be slaughtered by the beast or antichrist.</u>
2. This actually explains why God's wrath is released in the last days.
3. Millions will be slain; a great holocaust/genocide.

Notice these things:

    a. The martyred believers will be on the sea of glass.
    b. This sea of glass stretches before the throne of God Revelation 4:6: we read the victory before we ever became the victim in the previous verse in the fourth chapter!

1. This actually symbolizes the fire of persecution that the believers endured
2. The fire of the judgment that the evil ones are in store for.

    c. The martyred believers will be victorious over the antichrist:

    –   They will not worship his image: Rev. 13:15
    –   Will not ascertain his mark: Rev. 13: 16, 17

True believers will not follow the antichrist.

Noticed what is in the hands of those who are on and in the sea of glass; HARPS.

Consider the imagery here: Fire, Glass, and Harps.

- The Fire is for restitution, the glass is for reflection, and the harps are for restoration.

- Look again; harps were created to soothe those who have been troubled. (Do you remember when the King was troubled and sent for David to play a harp to calm him down?)
- In other words, he gives those who have been wronged something to soothe themselves and encourage their own selves.
- He then gives them the sheet music for their praise and worship service.

   – He says they sang a certain song in the midst of the fire and glass; it was the same song Moses' and his company sang as they crossed the Red sea.

1. Do you see the metaphors and imagery here?

   a. RED sea, (fire)
   b. SEA (sea of glass-reflection)
   c. It looked as though the enemy had won but there was the other side of the story.
   d. Then the record says: Then Moses sang! There ought to be a song when he saves!
   e. They actually sang an a and b selection: the song of Moses and the song of the Lamb

STOP HERE

   – A sign of seven plagues that are said to be the last plagues
   – A sign of God's wrath

Revelation 15:5

I.   Judgment of God

1. The door of the temple of the tabernacle is opened. (verse 5)
2. This place is the same as what they called the Holy of Holies/Most Holy Place in the Old Testament.

- This is the tabernacle of the testimony which is where the Ark of Covenant is here; hence combining the names (Ten Commandments and other contents; Aaron's rod, pot of manna, two tables, and anointing oil and other contents).
- Tabernacle means the dwelling place of God.
- You see this is the place where the beauty of God's holiness would consume is on anyone who entered.

3. The judgment of God will come and flow from the Holiest of places.
4. It will flow from the heart of God!

   a. In other words: his presence and heart will have been violated and polluted by the sin and evil committed.
   b. So vindication of his heart and presence will be received.

- Consider the scene:

- They are holding seven plagues in their hands
- They are dressed in pure and white linen- which is the symbol of holiness
- They have gold belts- which is the symbol of royalty and authority and power; he can execute justice when he decides to do so.

- The seven angels are given seven bowls that are FILLED with the wrath of God (verse 7).

- The bowl's whole imagery is about bowls not having a lid.
- There is no covering on the bowls: bowls like saucers for drinking and used for sacrifices; they also held the incense that would burn in the temple.
- There will be no hindrance to pouring out his Wrath-Greek THY-MOS which is a flash of anger; uncontrollable anger.
- You see when there are lids you can pour without spilling-they were shallow bowl that were easily to empty.
- When there is no lid; the contents go everywhere!

- If you try and stop it; it will only result in it splashing; splashing causes it to go places it would not have gone before!
- Nothing will be able to stop the bowl judgments of God.

II.   The door of the temple was shut (verse 8)

1. The door to the temple of God; which is to Heaven and Salvation will no longer opened! (Story of Noah…)
2. No one will be able to enter Heaven any longer, NOT until the seven judgments are finished.

   a. The first time in history that Heaven's door will be closed and re-opened later!
   b. This is kind of scary and troubling thought, to know that those who attempt to enter Heaven will show up and there is a closed sign for a moment in time saying we'll be back later… but the truth is when the doors open back up it will not be for those who saw the closed sign only those to come after.
   c. Prayers for mercy will not avail anything!
   d. The antichrist and all of his followers will have wrath released upon them.

- Look how detailed and descriptive the scene is:
- The glory and power of God was shining brighter than the sun itself; it becomes frustrated and furious that smoke emits from their energy.
- The smoke from the glory of God does not allow anyone in the temple: No one will be able to enter the temple to make intercession!
- Exodus 40: 34,35
- This means that nothing can affect the outcome anymore; not even Jesus!
- Now what gave light will consume the evil of the earth.
- John 3:36, Ephesians 5:6.

Chapter 16

I.   The angels are released and the vials are poured out.

    1.   The first vial releases a great sore. (boils and blisters; ulcerous, festering and cancerous sore) verse 2

        a.   Noisome suggests that this is very painful and discomfort, and distraction.
        b.   These sores will be open and foul, painful and putrefying, ugly and repulsive, humiliating and embarrassing.
        c.   No relief from these sores; torture. Exodus 9: 8-11
        d.   Boils are caused by bad blood and reveal corruption in the system.
        e.   This is reserved for those with bad blood.

    2.   The second vial releases a trial upon the sea that turns into blood. (naval blood; of dead men) verse 3

        a.   This thought to be the Mediterranean Sea.
        b.   This is not healthy blood this is diluted and polluted blood. Contaminated.
        c.   If everything in the oceans and waters were dead, there would be a foul smell.
        d.   Sea creatures floating and decomposing.
        e.   All homes that were valuable which were ocean-side are now worth nothing.

    3.   The third vial releases blood upon the rivers and fountains. (References Exodus 7:20 as God inflicted upon the enemies of old He will do with the enemies of the modern times) verse 4-7

        a.   Fresh waters.
            1. No water for drinking.
            2. No water for washing or bathing

b. You thirsted over the blood of men; so I will quench your thirst; here it's blood to drink!

c. This is inland streams and springs.

d. Water purification systems will yield blood.

4. The fourth vial releases control over the sun and the sun is used as a gun to shoot great heat upon men. Verse 8-9

    a. This was literally hell on earth.

    b. It will not just be high temperatures they will be scorched or better yet burned.

    c. The scars will remain and last longer than the torture.

    d. They would not even repent even at such great discomfort.

    e. As a matter of fact, they blasphemed God the more and the more they do; the more intensified it becomes. Can you imagine heat matching your sin?

    f. Malachi 4: 1-2

    g. In Revelation this is not to make men repent but to make them blaspheme the name of God.

5. The fifth vial releases upon the throne of the beast. (Full of darkness: which means that there will be much confusion, dismay and distress) verse 10-11

    a. From one extreme to another; from heat too thick; pitch black darkness.

    b. Seat here means the throne and Revelation 13:4 he acted as if he was invincible and we find different.

    c. You voted for evil now you are stuck with evil.

    d. Exodus 10: 21-23

    e. They blamed their troubles on God only to find out they were related to the beast.

    f. The suffering form the hear, sores, thirst, filth, smell, pitch black darkness makes matters worse.

    g. It will become so bad they will begin chewing their tongues.

6. The sixth vial releases upon the river Euphrates and three unclean spirits come out of the mouth of the beast, dragon, and false prophet looking like frogs to gather all the kings of the world to do battle in a place named Armageddon. Verse 12-16

   a. The Euphrates River is the longest and most important river of western Asia; it is 1780 miles long anywhere from 300 to 1200 yards wide and 10 to 30 feet deep and this major body of water was dried up!
   b. This is one of the oldest rivers in the Bible.
   c. Genesis 2 in the Garden of Eden.
   d. Eastern border of European empires and eastern border of the future Israel.
   e. Battle of Armageddon- the kings of the east: Palestine, Arabirabs, China and all other eastern nations; they will perhaps be led by Antichrist.
   f. The kings of the north are nations north of Palestine including Russia
   g. The kings of south: the nations of Africa.
   h. The kings of the west: western alliances, European nations, America, Canada and others.

7. The seventh vial releases upon the air and follows earthquakes, thunder, lightning, and great hail that weighs a talent. Verse 17-21

   a. The very air that mankind breathes is now affected; it is poisoned.
   b. Thunder and lightning normally warn that a great storm is coming.
   c. No earthquake can top this seismic seizure.
   d. It was so bad mountains disappeared nationally.
   e. Talent 75-100 pounds falling from the sky. The law of gravity falling from a never-ending sky.
   f. While a quarter-inch sphere of ice has a terminal velocity of 500 mph; such just imagine something that is less than an

ounce compared to something that is 100 pounds it would fall at approximately 8 million miles per hour.

g. Leviticus 24:16 says that the blasphemer should be stoned; and now they are stoned from Heaven.

- Seventh SEAL" reveals the events that are about to happen; the blast of the "Seventh TRUMPET" announces the events as forthcoming, and the outpouring of the "Seventh VIAL" executes them.
- When the seventh seal was broken there was silence; but when the seventh trumpet and seventh vial was poured there was great voices in Heaven saying IT IS DONE- John 19:30!

Chapter 17

- This is all about false religion
- Religion introduced by deception

1. Angel revealed the truth of religious Babylon to John. Verse 1
2. Religious Babylon is a prostitute. Verse 1
3. Religious Babylon sits on many waters (people). Verse 1
4. Religious Babylon will be supported by the nations and people of the world. Verse 2
5. Religious Babylon will receive power from the beast and antichrist. Verse 3
6. Religious Babylon will appear to be rich but in fact be corrupt. Verse 4
7. Religious will be prejudice. Verse 6

- Keep in mind that John is envisioning the last days of human existence.
- He has just witnessed Armageddon.
- All of the sudden an angel comes to him and this is one who poured wrath on the earth.
- The angel says to John; COME HERE!
- When he comes he is shown the judgment of the false religion.

- Religious Babylon is described as a prostitute (In the Bible being labeled a harlot is symbolic of false gods).
- Idolatry- having anything other than God become first and foremost in devotion.

    a. When a person imagines and thinks about what God is like and decides to follow their own thoughts and ideologies against that which they know is right and the scripture reveals.
    b. When they follow earthly religion and its rituals, and practices, ceremonies, and other practices against following the scriptures.

1. <u>Programmatic annuals</u>
2. <u>Liturgical dedications</u>
3. <u>We have never done things on that order</u>
4. <u>We wear certain garments</u>; (pants are repulsive for women, arms out, other denominations highlight no make-up, no stockings, no movies, etc.)
5. <u>When they mold and make an image and worships it.</u> (Cars-washing and always showing more interest there, Homes-mowing and manicuring, sports- hunting, fishing, trial riding, etc.)

- Deception- sits on many waters which suggests that it will take place in many races, languages and nations.

1. Millions will follow this false religion, but more importantly; think about how many profess Christ but do not truly believe and actually practice the practices of Christ!
2. Verse 2 says that religious Babylon will be supported by kings (governments)! WOW! The governments will support exercising and encourage false god worship!

    a. Homosexuality/Lesbianism.
    b. Keep the poor; poor.
    c. Promote racism.

3. Notice how the government will support those who are part of Religious Babylon; in other words, if we would just acquiesce to their standards and practices we will be supported.

   a. Socially- You will be accepted by a community that otherwise would not accept you
   b. Economically- There will be means made to cause you to thrive in businesses
   c. Politically- Your pull in what you can speak for and against is laid before you
   d. Financially- Unlimited resources

   – It says they will become drunk on the wine of false teaching.
   – When you are drunk; you cannot think for yourself
   – You cannot function
   – You cannot travel
   – You cannot make conscious decisions

   • People desire to be a part of a religion whereas they can belong that permits worldliness and does not teach/Preach separation form the world!
   • Equality with women's movements; equality with homosexuality/lesbianism: how can anything be labeled as equal when God said it's wrong!
   • It is an abomination and must be viewed and spoken as of such.

   – In verse 3 it states that Religious Babylon sits upon a scarlet colored beast. (Sitting represents being supported upon the state.
   – The scarlet colored beast is the antichrist.
   – The seven heads- seven nations that will voluntarily surrender to the control of the antichrist.
   – The nations under control will be the primary nations preaching the false religion of Babylon.

   1. Revelation 13 helps us with this as part of our research of the seven heads as well as Daniel 7

2. Babylon-the lion, Persia- the bear, Greece- the four headed leopard, Turkey, Syria- Assyria, Egypt, Rome.

Revelation 17:4

- Purple and scarlet clothing has to do with being extremely wealthy and false religion.
- There are greater than 40,000 people who die from hunger every day and these people in this false religion are rich with everything they need!
- The name of the false religion is: MYSTERY!
- Many people will be worshipping a false religion and not even know it.

1. Following a religion and people who they are unaware of that is a religion other than God!

- Religious Babylon will be the Mother of many false religions
- She will give birth to many different ideologies
- Tower Of Babel (Genesis 11) The leader is named Nimrod
- They figured they could build a stairway and tower to Heaven
- They were dependent upon their own strength rather than GOD!
- Babel is the founding of the city of Babylon! <u>(Wow; it is actually the root word of Babylon)</u>

   a. Bah-bell which means to confuse. בָּבֶל it actually means to mix; this is actually one of the places in scripture whereas cultural language walks hand in hand with cultural genetic mixture! Because they scattered to different places of the earth. Strong's Talking Greek & Hebrew Dictionary.

- <u>The name Babylon actually means: godless religion</u>
- <u>It can also mean: godless government and society!</u>

1. Babylon and false religion is every effort that seeks after:
- Man's work
- Man's goodness

- Man's rituals
- Man's own ideas and worship of God
- Man's own religion

- You see the only way to reach Heaven is through Jesus Christ and not by man made efforts!
- When people believe and still honor leaders, governments, states, doctrines, and rituals and traditions over God it is a mystery!
- It is hypocrisy
- Jim Crow, David Koresh, Muslim, Atheism, Hinduism, etc. they share their beliefs at the expense of others and in the strength of one person.
- Verses 13 and 14 speaks about the ideology of the other religions: they will have one mind; they will not think and research for themselves outside of the box, they will be stuck with one thought and it is an IMPOSED thought. Otherwise a forced reality!

The following are examples of those who will oppose the cross (verse 14)
    a. They reject the cross being the only way
    b. They do not resolve that Jesus' death paid for our sins
    c. Christ was a mere mortal man

- Once the power and loyalty of the people the antichrist will no longer need the religion!
- Religious Babylon will be destroyed by the Antichrist; being that the Antichrist destroys Religious Babylon, this happens in order to accrue its wealth and power.
- So the very thing you fought and believed in will destroy you for everything you worked to make happen. (Verse 16)
- They would have fought each other in the end!
- God plants into the mind of the antichrist to strip Religious Babylon of everything and leaver the whore/harlot naked and exposed!
- The only Religion that will be left standing will be Christianity.

Revelation 18

- This deals with the destruction of political Babylon.
- This is the capital of the antichrist (Revelation 14:8)
- This could metaphorically be speaking of any great city beginning to fall who were actually godless: D.C., New York, Moscow, London, Paris

1. In verse 1 there is the angelic announcement

   a. The angel lined in glory and lights up the whole earth; this is to say that the announcement is so important; the whole earth needs to listen.

2. Verses 2-7 the reason why Babylon will be destroyed is disclosed

Verse 4 says: when you have intercourse with her it would mean sharing the plague and pain with everybody you come into contact with.

Verse 5 says: her sins are piled up to heaven. They think their sins are going unnoticed by God. They practice their sins openly.

   a. There are five reasons this city will be destroyed.
   b. Spiritual corruption; a place where satan occupies, demonic spirits prevail
   c. Listen to the imagery given concerning the reasoning
   d. The cage for every hateful and unclean bird

1. Immorality, fornication, adultery, homosexuality, abnormal sex
2. Lying, stealing, cheating will run ramped
3. Lusting after more of possessions
4. Sorcery, devil worship, witchcraft, palm readers, fortune tellers, astrology
5. Secularism, materialism, humanism will dominate people

- There are multiple spirits that corrupt mankind

THE SPIRIT OF BONDAGE
Romans 8:15

THE SPIRIT OF THE WORLD
I Corinthians 2:12

THE SPIRIT OF MAN
I Corinthians 2:11

THE SPIRIT THAT WORKS IN CHILDREN OF DISOBEDIENCE
Ephesians 2:2

THE SPIRIT OF FALSE TEACHING AND PREACHING
I John 4:1

THE SPIRIT OF ERROR
I John 4:6

- Babylon is being destroyed because she has corrupted: nations, kings, and all people.
- See the word fornication in this text alludes to spiritual fornication; the rejection of God and turning to other gods.
- Secularism (political or social policy that reject any religious faith), humanism (Human interests dominate), and materialism (preoccupation with materialistic items) is when man begins to surround and focus his life around…

    – Technology
    – Science
    – Education
    – Pleasures
    – Recreation
    – Comforts
    – ABORT the very thing that has the potential to produce LIFE!

    a. Secularism offers everything a person desires except Christ…
       II Timothy 3: 1-2-II Timothy 4:3

    b. Verse 6 reveals that this Babylonian people will have a place in persecuting the saints; because the scripture says: SHE REWARDED YOU!

3. Verse talks about how quick it will happen; ONE DAY

  – It is said to be a plague released and has the same effect of a poisonous gas.

4. Verses 9-20 speaks about the severity and how impactful the fall will be

  – Verse 17a says that the businessmen will mourn and then notice the word: SLAVERY.
  – In other words, people will not mean anything but a number to the leaders

- Slaves to debt
- Slaves to lenders
- Refinancing at higher rates, credit cards, etc.
- Through commerce
- Average interest rate for payday/title loans is 391% to 521%
- Buy, sell and trade athletes
- Slaves to our jobs
- Human trafficking

5. Verses 21-23 the actual destruction of Babylon

  – Notice the strength of the angel with the boulder
  – The velocity in the throwing of the boulder
  – Impact of the boulder on the water
  – How quickly the boulder disappears
  – Water goes in every direction
  – This will be the culmination of the destruction; IT IS ALMOST AS IF THERE IS AN EXPLOSION WITH THIS BOULDER. So will Babylon be; SEEN NO MORE!

6. Verses 23 and 24 repeats why they will be destroyed

Revelation 19

– This is the great wedding supper of the Lamb.
– All of Heaven will be present to witness the marriage of Christ and the believers who have followed Him.
– This will be the most celebrated event in history.

• The wedding supper will be filed with glorious praise
• The wedding supper will focus on the Lamb
• The wedding supper will produce a pure bride
• The wedding supper will be a glorious event

The praise is centered on four hallelujahs in verses: 1,3,4,6.

Hallelujah really means praise GOD.

a. Alleluia in Hebrew derives from two words: <u>halal</u> which means praise and <u>jah</u> which is the name of God.
b. This supper will be the hallelujah for salvation to be made pure.
c. Glory alone belongs to God. All the glory.
d. Honor belongs to God. (He will be honored as the source and creator at the wedding supper.) Revelation 19:7 honour means: glory, praise and worship

– The supper will be filled with hallelujah for victory! Verses 2-3

1. Jesus will triumph over all of the evil of the earth.
    a. Godless politics- social, commercial, cultural, and religious
    b. He will avenge the persecution and abuse of followers. He will judge and destroy every evil, abusive, murdering, person

• In most weddings/wedding receptions the focus is placed upon the bride but this supper the focus is on the groom!

    a.   If Jesus is the focus at this occasion; how much more true should it be for today?

    b.   All of our attention; on the contrary we want the attention and he gets none! Luke 9:23; Romans 12:1

1. The bride (church) prepares herself as a bride does.
2. The bride wants to prepare herself to be acceptable to the groom!
3. We prepare ourselves by accepting the Lamb and following the Lamb.

Revelation 20

  – Satan being removed and bound!

  – Jesus will return to earth and to eliminate all ungodliness and evil within the earth.

- This is when the earth will know no more sin
- No more rejection denial or cursing God or Jesus
- No more sickness or death
- No more murder

I.   <u>This is the kingdom of God coming to earth.</u>

1. This is when the earth will revert back to being the Garden of Eden again. The only difference is it will be better than it once was. The questions concerning satan's removal

    a.   Who will remove him? The angel of God verses 1 and 2

1. The angel notice is leaving directly from the presence of God.
2. Angel means aggelon which is interpreted messenger.
3. A messenger form Heaven will remove satan.
4. Consider that this angel has keys. (Matthew 16:19, Revelation 1:18)
5. The angel has two things in his hands: the keys to the bottomless pit; the abyss and a great chain; to bind satan up.
6. Who can bind satan up and remove him other than God?

    b.   Who is satan? The dragon/old serpent verse 2

1. His very name tells us who he is!
2. The old serpent; the one who deceives and seduces (Garden of Eden terminology again)

    c. How long will satan be removed? 1,000 years' verse 2

1. No more wars/killing
2. Crimes will be eradicated
3. No hunger or homelessness
4. No more laziness
5. No more drugs enslavement or drunkenness
6. This will be a place of utopia!

    d. Where will satan be placed? The abyss verse 3
    e. Will satan be released? For a short time, verse 3

1. As of right now let's consider the idea of satan being removed; SIN tastes good, looks good, and feels good.
2. Consider things that fit this category:

- Food
- Sex
- Honor
- Recognition
- Vehicles
- Money
- Pleasure
- Power
- Clothes
- Houses
- Possessions
- Fleshly stimulations
- Popularity
- Position
- Comfort

None of these are wrong; many are necessary for life the lusting after these are wrong.

- To lust after more and more food
- Lust after another person
- Lust after power others possess
- Lust after pleasure and possessions
- Lust after position and money

When satan is to be removed there will no deception and power struggles His Kingdom will have come and we live in a place of utopia!

1. There will be a change in earth; Isaiah 35: 1,2
2. There will be a shift in the animal kingdom; Isaiah 11: 6-9 (Message Bible)
3. There will be change in the process of life; Isaiah 35: 5,6

Revelation 20: 4-6

- This is the great millennial reign of Christ on earth. (Millennial simply means one thousand years)
- Christ is returning to earth as the conquering Saviour and defeats and destroys the antichrist and beasts during Armageddon and the removal of satan during the millennial reign.

I.   There is the resurrection of the believers in verse 4

   a. John sees thrones and people sitting on them and ability to judge and rule.
   b. He sees the martyred believers during tribulation.
   c. Who are the people sitting on the thrones?

1. They are those who come to life and reign with Christ.
2. They are those who take place in the first resurrection. (believers who have died)
3. He mentions the martyrs separately because they paid the ultimate price for the cause of Christ.

4. They died for Him.
5. This appointment is when Jesus gives us our eternal assignments and duties. Judgment was given unto them (This could be enlarged later on when the new Heavens and the new earth is created)
6. Satan is removed from power. Satan is dethroned.

II. The millennial reign of Christ will only see resurrection of believers. Verse 5

    a. Millennial reign-believers; martyrs-1,000 years
    b. 1st resurrection: after millennial reign-unbelievers
    c. There will be one thousand years between the first and second resurrections.
    d. 1st resurrection is for the believers and the second is for the unbelievers
    e. The resurrection does not pertain at all to those who are still will still be upon the earth.

1. The resurrected believers have six privileges:

    a. <u>Extremely blessed</u>: makarios joy and satisfaction being complete and fulfilled.
    b. <u>Holy</u>: perfectly separated from the world; we will then have the very same nature of Christ
    c. <u>Never be touched by the second death-</u> this is a different kind of death. Separated from God forever. Cast into the lake of fire.
    d. <u>We will serve as a priest of God and Christ</u> no need for a mediator. The only difference between now and then is we then stand face to face with God. Now we can only approach Him through prayer and thought.
    e. <u>We rule and reign with Christ.</u> II Timothy 2:12- read it in the Message Bible!

1. Our salvation hinges on this principle! The only way and place to reign is to be in Christ in Heaven.

2. This suggests that the members will be treated as the head. We have major misconceptions with this practice.
3. We must practice this on earth in order to experience it in Heaven.
4. This is true dogma (doctrine). Theory, theoretical, belief
5. The word suffer in the text is transliterated as the word: endure etymologically has a dual meaning: it means to last and to go through suffering; PATIENTLY.
6. SUFFER WITH WHAT? Shame, reproach, loss of goods, loss of credit, punishment, abused, even death.
7. This is why I have ceased allowing people, church folk and others to discourage me so when they do not do what I know God has said to do. I WANT TO REIGN WITH HIM.
8. My reigning there is not worth giving that up just to reign here!

    f.   <u>We serve under the rule of Christ</u>

Revelation 20: 7-16

I.   This is somewhat troubling; satan is about to be set free; he has made bail; he is being released.

1. He is now being allowed to deceive people again.
2. Why?

    a.   He will be released to deceive for the very same reason he is permitted to tempt us now! (To show man what is in his heart and to show man that he needs to turn to God)

    b.   Everyone in the earth during the millennium will not be saved and will be given chance.

Revelation 21: 1-8

    – This is now all about eternity.
    – Forever and ever
    – All of the bad and negative things will now be all in the past.
    – Pollution, impurities and ungodliness will be no more.

1. Impure government
2. Corrupt religion
3. Terrible leaders
4. Painful suffering
5. Sin and temptation

- Listen to what we have said and now will become the reality:

1. No more tears
2. No more sorrow
3. No more crying
4. No more pain
5. No more death

- New Heaven and New Earth

1. New creation verse 1

   a. Everything will be new: earth, moon, stars, planets, everything will be destroyed and remade.
   b. Think about this no more typhoons, earthquakes any of this.
   c. We look up at the stars and moon and look up and say that is beautiful; it has nothing on the new heaven and earth.
   d. Nothing burns down, out or up.
   e. Consider the earth; it is infected now, it is defective: volcanic eruptions, storms, floods, ice storms, etc.
   f. Roses will exist without thorns; anything that is planted will grow because all soil will be fertile, every day will be clear.
   g. No more hunger, or thirst.
   h. Grass will always be green, trees will never die, streets will never crack, bees will never sting, snakes cannot attack, food will never ruin.

- New Jerusalem verse 2

   a. This is the thought of the capital city in Heaven
   b. It symbolizes the very presence of God.

    c.   The Lord's throne will sit in the midst of New Jerusalem

    d.   The city comes down from Heaven; it is not built on earth but is transported from Heaven to earth.

    e.   Likened as a bride adorned for her husband

    f.   A bride wants to be beautiful and be in the presence of her groom; the church desires to look her best and spend the rest of our lives with him…till death do us part; OH WAIT. There is no death.

2.   Immediate fellowship with God in verse 2

    a.   It is like this when the holy city is moved here; then and only then will God's presence and glory will dwell here on earth.

    b.   The longing of our heart is built to long for Him.

1.   Four things happen: tabernacle of God will be with men
2.   God will dwell with them
3.   They will be his people
4.   He will be their God

3.   Perfection of everything verses 4-6

    a.   Our bodies will be perfected

1.   No more aging
2.   No more miscarriages
3.   Dying children
4.   Hearse wheels rolling
5.   No more disappointment (crying)
6.   The former things are passed away

4.   Citizens of Heaven verses 6-8

    a.   Instead of telling us who it will be; He tells us who it will NOT be!

    b.   those who continued in their sins will be rejected of Christ verse 8

1. Fearful- cowardly: scared of what others might say; those who cannot give up the world
2. unbelieving- those do not believe
3. Abominable or polluted- worldly people, those who touch and taste impurities, they are contaminated. Colossians 2:21 this is all about people who set all kind of rules that have nothing to do with nothing!
4. Murderers- those who kill and then those who destroy lives; marriages, relationships, alternative lifestyles, sexual abuse, and many others methods.
5. Whoremongers or immoral- fornicators, adulterers, homosexuality, lesbianism, bi-sexual, tri-sexual (Anybody or anything; no preference)
6. Sorcerers- those who partake in astrology, witchcraft, devil worship, séances, palm reading, fortune telling, tarot cards etc.
7. Idolaters- worshippers of idols whether it is in a person's hands or mind.
8. Liars- prevaricators and fabricators.

Revelation 21: 9-23

- <u>The mentioning of the capital city.</u>

– The New Jerusalem Revelation 21:2, 3:12
– The Heavenly Jerusalem Hebrew 12:22
– The Holy City Revelation 21:2, 21: 19
– Holy Jerusalem Revelation 21:10
– The City of my God Revelation 3:12
– The Great City Revelation 21:10

I. What will be the likes of this city?

    a. What words could describe a city of God when He created everything?
    b. God possesses the intelligencia and power and this city exudes of who He is.

    c.   How could our language or linguistics explain what the contents of this city shall be?

    d.   Well, this is the issue John ran into; attempting to explain New Jerusalem.

    e.   John used the best of the best words to describe what he saw

    f.   Verses 9 and 10 speaks about the last vision given to John

1. God sends one of the seven angels who cast one of the bowls judgments upon the earth to take John on the tour.
2. The symbolism here is: that there is not only judgment but there is hope and citizenship is available.

    g.   Verse 11 speaks about the glory of the city

1. The glory of God gives light to the city
2. If you have ever seen an actual scene of everything in a setting of a mountain being covered by snow and seemed surreal this is the offering of seeing a crystal ice palace.
3. Everything sparkles and glitters; trees, bushes, branches, blades of grass.
4. Imagine how beautiful it would be to see the green jasper ricocheting off of the ice crystals. Luke 2:9

    h.   Verse 12 speaks about the high walls of the city

1. This is a picture of security; form what you might ask? It is just a symbolism that no more will there be anything to worry about

    i.   Verses 12 and 13 speaks of the twelve gates

1. The gates have the names of the twelve tribes; this symbolizes that the only way to get to God would be through the God of one of the twelve tribes. John 4:22
2. The gates ae guarded by 12 angels; symbolizes the city is protected by angels as security at the gates; no person can enter the city unless they are approved and names are on the list

3. Entrances in every direction; symbolizes everybody on earth is invited discrimination or prejudices

    j. Verse 14 speaks of the foundations; and the names of the apostle's inscriptions

1. They are deemed as apostles of the Lamb; a believer must build their lives upon the testimony that Jesus is Lord

    k. Verse 15-17 speaks of the shape and size of the city

1. The city is square
2. The city is enormous; 1500 miles long, wide, and high: This is 2 and one quarter million square miles or 3 billion 375 million cubic miles.
3. The city has thick walls; 144 cubits; which is translated to 216 feet thick (verse 17)

    l. Verse 18-21 speaks about the material of the city; being precious and priceless

1. The valued stones and materials are much different than what we know
2. Walls made of jasper; crystal like stone made of a green material
3. City is made of pure gold that is clear as glass; all this city made of PURE Gold; this gives a new rise to pure gold
4. Twelve foundations are bedazzled with every kind of stone

    a. 1st foundation made of jasper
    b. 2nd foundation is sapphire (sky blue spotted with gold)
    c. 3rd foundation is chalcedony (a green like that of a peacock's tail)
    d. 4th is emerald (the greenest of all greens)
    e. 5th is sardonyx (different shades of color)
    f. 6th is sardius (a blood red stone)
    g. 7th is chrysolite (shining stone with gold radiance)
    h. 8th is beryl (sea blue/sea green stone)

    i.   9th is topaz (greenish gold stone)

    j.   10th is chrysoprasus (an apple green stone)

    k.   11th is jacinth (violet bluish-purple stone)

    l.   12th is amethyst (violet, bluish-purple but more brilliant than the jacinth)

    m.   13th is the twelve gates are lined in pearls

Verse 22 speaks about the city worship and how it focuses on God himself

1.   There is no temple/church in Heaven
2.   Every person will be filled with the Holy Spirit (Much different than here)
3.   They will be perfectly filled; Holy Ghost Takeover; completely controlled
4.   Worship will never cease; because we will ever have on our mind that we are in the very presence of God continuously.
5.   Unbroken fellowship; no need for temples/ritualistic ceremonies: these things are to engage the minds of humans.

    a.   No need for priming, pumping, prepping and etc. we are IN THE PRESENCE. Jon 4:24, II Corinthians 10:5, Isaiah 26:3

    m.   Verse 23 speaks about the city light; the glory of God and the lamb

Revelation 22: 1-21

- There is a pure river in the city; and it possesses the water of life.
- With Heaven 1500 square miles that is a lot of water.
- The water symbolizes our thirst quenched. John 4:10

1.   There is then mentioned the Tree of Life- now remember this Tree was planted in the Garden of Eden! Genesis 2:9
2.   Here it is now mentioned again in the last chapter of Revelation.
3.   As long as man was sinless he was allowed to eat of this tree, but it was not until sin crept in that he was not allowed to eat of the tree at all!

4. The fruit gave nourishment, nutriment, life.
5. It was actually infusing eternal life into Adam.

    a. The Tree of Life has twelve crops of fruit.
    b. One for each month.
    c. You missed it; the tree bear fruit year round.
    d. This principle states that there is no stop, only continuous life there.
    e. It is eternal fruit and the person who eats it becomes eternal.

6. The leaves are good for the healing of the nations.

    a. They provide for a perfect life; no hindrances, no imperfections.
    b. The leaves prevent sickness and illnesses.
    c. They produce a perfect body.

II.   There is no more curse in the city

1. The earth has been cursed!

    a. Aging
    b. Corruption
    c. Deterioration
    d. Decay
    e. Death
    f. Suffering
    g. Evil
    h. Division
    i. Disasters

2. Man made this decision when he decided to do things his way other than God's way.
3. He says that his word (verse 6) is faithful and true.

    a. In other words; you can depend on this.

4. The seventh verse says; he who readeth this book shall be blessed.

5. We must also study and obey this book.

6. Because as we have read and studied this book it should have drawn us closer to God.

7. How so; it changed the sense of urgency and made it more urgent.

8. Notice why he says that we should read and obey this word; because I come quickly. I John 2:3 Message

9. When John heard these things he was overwhelmed with a spirit of Worship.

   a. This is the second time John was rebuked for worshipping an angel.

   b. The angel who was delivering the message had to correct him.

   c. The point is this: when we study Revelation it should drive us to want to worship God more and more; BUT we should make certain that we should worship the only True and living God.

10. He said that his is book is to never be sealed.

    a. In other words, never close the book;
    b. Preach it
    c. Sing it
    d. Live it
    e. Walk it
    f. Study it
    g. Pray it
    h. Show it
    i. Share it
    j. Many of us have closed the book!

11. The only way to partake in this city is for your robe to be washed; in the blood; not keep his commandments.

III. THE Word of God is not to be messed with verses 18 and 19

   1. If he adds; the plagues will be added to him and every other curse.
   2. If he takes away God will take his share in the tree of life.
   3. Adding to make your message be heard
   4. Taking away that which does not satisfy your spiritual palate.

Lesson Twelve

"Tips For Talking By Faith"
Proverbs 15:1

Have you ever tried to argue in a whisper?
It is hard to argue with someone who insists on answering softly.
A rising voice triggers an angry response.

Grievous – means as is moldering fire is excited.

The man who controls his tongue shows that he has his personal emotions under subjection (Faith).

"A gentle answer will calm a person's anger, but an unkind answer will cause more anger." Proverbs 15:1 (NCV)

We tend to "talk back" to those who speak to us in anger. Part defense mechanism, part pride, the Bible teaches this usually doesn't work.

We can become more effective at positive conversation if we will maturely swallow our pride and respond to a heated barb with a kind and calm answer.

We may need to empathize with the angry person. Why are they behaving so drastically? They may have a hurt that we can help heal.

Being kind and calm does not mean that we cannot be firm and truthful. But angry exchanges seldom accomplish the peace of God.

SEEK FIRST TO UNDERSTAND, THEN TO BE UNDERSTOOD.

This is actually habit 5 of Stephen Covey's "7 Habits of Highly Effective People", but it is certainly Bible-based.

In Covey's book, he mentions the 5 levels of listening: 1) Ignoring; 2) Pretending (to listen); 3) Selective Listening; 4) Attentive Listening; and 5) Empathetic Listening.

(Pages 240-241, "The 7 Habits of Highly Effective People")

"Don't use foul or abusive language. Let everything you say be good and helpful, so that your words will be an encouragement to those who heal them." Ephesians 4:29 (NLT)

Tip # 1 for talking in Faith our reception is bad.
(Before cable television came to be, folk used what they called an antenna, one day a man had problems with his reception and television, and the worker came out and said your signal is strong, but your antenna is not pointed in the right direction.)

So the word of God is strong.

No problem with the signal, our hearts antenna is often not pointed in the right direction.

We move it our spiritual antennas around hoping to fix the reception, change channels seeming to wish for a better picture, but forget that they needed to be pointed toward God.

- If they hit you hit them back- parents
- If they call you a name, right back at them.
- If they do something to you get them back.

We have to learn how to be God-inspired!

II Timothy 3:16

Let's talk about this word inspiration.

All scriptures are given by the inspiration of God.
The Greek word for inspiration here is theopneustos.

Made up of two words.

The word for God and a word that means to breathe out, or exhale.

So all scriptures are the exhaling of God.

We have watered down this word inspiration.

- Does not mean that choir was inspirational
- That preacher's message inspired me.
- Did you see that young man/woman that sure did inspire me?

Watch this even though it has been delivered by many authors it was inspired of God.

Remember as we were growing up; your mama or daddy would say go tell your brother/sister I said to do this or do that.

You would leave and say mama/daddy said, that was a voice of authority.

It did not mean you had authority over your siblings. But once you said mama/daddy said it carried weight.

So if your brother or sister disobeys your words, your parents view it as disobeying them directly.

But if you change up what was initially said you would be in trouble because you took authority that was not yours.

The Greek word pheromenoi, translated moved, means to be carried or driven along, like winds driving the sails of a ship.

Otherwise where God speaks inspiration on me, he pheromenoi- moves me to where I need to go and what I need to say because my thoughts and my speech are not my words but his words.

Now listen if we are to talk by faith it means that what we say ought not be what we know to say but what we depend on Him to say through us.

It gets deep watch this, many of times when I counsel, encourage, pray, and/or preach I do not know what I am to say until I talk by faith, which is to say not know what He wants me to say until he moves me to say it.

I hope I'm making sense here, far too often we mess up b trying to make our words be His words, and then what we do is misrepresent Him by concluding that we are saved and then say unsaved words!

I said something you just missed it.

It's like this if I feel like saying it is the wrong thing to say, because my words are detrimental, think back to Proverbs 15:1 be careful what you say because it is explosive, it is destructive, it is demonstrative.

Our problem as believers is we say the wrong thing because we don't trust that what God wants us to say will work.

- – If I let them get away, they'll think they can do every time.
- – If I do not let them have it, they might think they can run over me.

- • We premise our oratorical endeavors on how much a person knows or their social order, but this scripture clearly and plainly states that when you talk to someone your mindset should be excused.

Because we have read that without faith it is impossible to please God.

Otherwise if I cannot trust Him enough in my speech, I become displeasing in His presence.

I must understand that what I say is a direct reflection on what I say he gave me!

Let me go a step further when I speak certain ways to certain people it says that what I say is what God breathed or inspired me to say, because our words can either stir up anger or turn away wrath; question is which one are we guilty of.

I know it's a hard one to answer honestly but are we peacemakers by way of our tongue, or those who stir things up.

If we are the one's stirring up things, then we in essence are displeasing to God. And those who are displeasing to God are not welcomed in His presence.

See you are not trusting God when you match what God says against your reason, and your reason wins.

Or when you match what God says against your feelings, and your feelings win.

Or when you match God's words against your conscience and your conscience wins. That's not talking by faith.

Talking by faith means to sometimes go against your reason, your feelings, and your conscience, everything you were raised to believe.

There are a lot of talkers in and around the churches today that have not matched what they are saying to what God word says.

Tip #2 for talking by faith be sure of what you see and hear.
James 1: 22-25

Watch how James puts this the person he says that is in the mirror in Greek means a male, peculiar, which would be opposed to male and female.

For one; men don't spend much time in the mirror, follow me here.

We tend to glance in the mirror and go on. Whereas women study their appearance.

So James says don't just look into the word and go on, the way a man does and not notice what needs to be hanged.

Ok what are mirrors designed to do?

They are made to show us exactly what we look like so that we might see what is wrong and correct it.

The mirror only reflects what is there. So we cannot get upset with the outcome, because the mirror tells the truth.

You see what happens is many people mark their bibles but their bibles never mark them.

What we do is we use the word as chewing gum.

Watch this, we chew it until the flavor is gone, then we spit it out, until we can get a fresh piece of gum, or scripture that is nice and juicy.

Many of Christians like good sermons, had a few hear tell me so.

But they ignore the word until they hear something else that excites them.

Sometimes I am even asked, "What are you going to preach next?"

It seems as if that person or persons has chewed on the last sermon, got the entire flavor out of it, wadded it up and threw it away. Now it's time for a new piece.

Do you know you can never grow if you only chew food, the growth and nutrition comes for digesting the food?

It's amazing the way women use mirrors; they want a 360 degree look.

Then if that is not bad enough they pull out another mirror, and look at the back to take another look.

In other words, they are looking intently into the mirror. They want to cover all ground. They do not want to miss anything, because they want to look their best.

Let's continue with James 1: 26-27

The word religion in this passage has to do with our external spiritual activity.

Those things that others can see or hear us doing.

James is saying that genuine faith ought to produce genuine works.

If you cannot bridle your tongue, there must be the absence of faith.

Watch this, turn to James 3:9

He says we bless God on Sunday, and then turn around and curse our brothers and sisters on Monday which are made similar to God.

Then he asks a very pertinent question in the 11th verse.

Lesson Thirteen

"United or Untied"
Psalm 133: entirety

Read a picture that stated: teamwork is what makes the team work...

Living in unity does not mean we will agree on everything.
But we must agree on our purpose to work together for God.

Behold- Look, not listen how good it is, because that would have left a loop hole for us.
Behold, how good and how pleasant it is for brethren to dwell together in unity! It is the characteristic of real saints

He says stop pause and gaze look upon it.

I CORINTHIANS 14:33
Philippians 4:7

He uses how twice.

He uses these two adjectives; good and pleasant
Watch this he says it's good
We often find things that are good
But to tack on that it is pleasant makes it better.

You see when you separate it, it weakens.
To have things that are a pleasure, sometimes are evil.

Dwell- that is where you live; not where you may stop, otherwise it is how you are 24-7.

It is like the precious oil upon the head,
(It cools the scorching heat of men's passions, as the dews cool the air and refresh the earth.)

Running down on the beard,
the beard of Aaron
Moses used this to anoint Aaron as the first high-priest of Israel.
Exodus 29:7

(Expensive oil was used by Moses to anoint Aaron as the 1st high priest of Israel.)

You see the ointment was Holy; so must our love for each other be holy.
Pure heart; devotion to God.
(How can love be Holy?)
Holiness is a lifestyle; therefore, Holy love is something that you live not something that falls from your lips.

Watch this Aaron and his sons were not permitted to minister until they were anointed with this ointment.
(Uh-oh you mean we cannot effectively witness or minister if we are not on the same page working together yes I am.)

Nor are our services acceptable to God.
Without this Holy love; if we don't have it we are nothing!
-it is fructifying, profitable, and fruit-bearing
Thus Holy love in the sight of God is precious.
(Precious- means something of great value or worth; much prized)

So in essence He is saying that when we genuinely get along it's something that God loves to watch.

Running down on the edge of his garments.
3 It is like the dew of Hermon

(Mount Hermon is the tallest mountain in Palestine, just north of the Galilean Sea)
Well, what does dew do?
It moistens the earth.
It makes it tender.
To receive the good seed.
(Spiritually word of God)

It has fertilizing power.
(FALLS ON THE GROUND IN ORDER TO PRODUCE LATER)

Likewise, does it our heart, but watch how he puts it he says it is like the dew of Hermon
Tallest mountain but it stays moist enough that when it hits the ground it still accomplishes what it set out to do.
(No matter how low you are brought down your deeds, expressions, hugs, handshakes, your smiles should help somebody else.)

You see Hermon and Mount Zion will wither without this dew
Micah 5:7
Our love should not tarry for theirs to us.

Otherwise don't just love somebody because they love you.
Indictment of the church.
-that is publican's love.
Publican-tax collector

If I may blow your mind real quick and share this with you;
Aaron was the pastor so to speak here the Holy Oil was poured on him first then ran down,

Watch me we are the Chosen people now, we are Zion, we are Aaron, if we can learn how to dwell in unity with the head, everything else will fall in place.

-Listen in order for the people to dwell together in unity it takes Aaron to start off with the oil running down.

(Otherwise I have to love unconditionally, and continuously.)

Secondly after I do that the word of God says their God will command His blessing.
(For one he says blessing- there's only but one.)

Then the b part to that is that when the head is blessed the rest of the body is blessed.

Descending upon the mountains of Zion; for there the LORD commanded the blessing—
Life forevermore.

Achieve Unity = Achieve Blessing
When we walk in unity we can accomplish supernatural achievements. We can walk on Water together.

- this mountain received very large amounts of water
- it seemed to be a source of moisture (provision) for the land below this is a visual example of how (in a similar way) the blessings of God flow to His People who are in unity and are obedient to Him.

He says as he closes THERE will the Lord command the blessing.

Watch this when he speaks of their background studies yield that there is in reference to Jerusalem.
(Where God dwells)

Therefore, where people dwell together in love he commands His blessing.
This is the blessing of blessings; He commands this blessing.
Not based on what you have asked for; it is based on how you have lived!!

What a blessing that is to be blessed according to how you live; you cannot fake this.

The enemy knows that if he can keep us in an uproar…up in arms against each other that we will be powerless against him…

Unity is the key to seeing souls saved...
Unity is the key to living in The Power of God
Unity is the key to being used by God...

God hates confusion and when we are not unified we cause confusion among our groups/church and then that is when we fight against what we believe in...The Kingdom of God is weakened by discord...
We must get serious and pray and speak against discord and confusion

We will get mad at somebody from the church and quit coming; or quit a ministry, or quit giving, or quit saying amen.

Well the question is
Who were you coming for in the 1st place?
Who were you working for?
Who were you giving to?
Why were you saying amen?

A few questions to write down and think over concerning this lesson!

What are some of the challenges of getting along with your family?

How has your relationship with others been affected by your faith in God? Vice-versa?

How do you think a Christian family might differ from a family who does not believe in the Lord?

Whoever loves his brother lives in the light, and there is nothing in him to make him stumble.
(1 John 2:10)

Blest be the tie that binds our hearts in Christian love! The fellowship of kindred minds is like to that above.
Before our Father's throne we pour our ardent prayers; our fears, our hopes, our aims are one, our comforts and our cares.

We share our mutual woes, our mutual burdens bear; and often for each other flows the sympathizing tear.

When we asunder part it gives us inward pain; but we shall still be joined in heart, and hope to meet again.

Lesson Fourteen

"Can't Been Dead A Long Time"
Philippians 4:13

I never realized until today at the conclusion of my studying this passage that there was credence and/or spiritual significance to this statement. (Expound)

No matter how severe the problem may be, we can.

As a matter of fact, the presidential campaign was littered with these words all throughout the process, because the message President Obama wanted to send was that no matter how difficult it may appear; we can.

Our overcoming is in the proclamation that we can!

You see Christ infuses us with strength when we declare I can.

There is literally power laced in the words I can, when tied to Him.

We hear periodically Lord give him/her more strength.

Good strength is not something that we need more of; we only are to be connected with him and we have all we need.

Otherwise our victory is in and through Him.

When Paul wrote this verse he had in mind physical things not spiritual things.

For we but work in the physical and expect God to work in the spiritual.

Think about it for a moment, we are physical, thereby we can only accomplish physical things being physical, but with Christ we are able to accomplish spiritual things.

Watch this, when Paul says;
I can do- Ischuo- means to be strong, to have power, or to have resources.

Otherwise here on earth I can do whatever the spiritual will allow me to do.

I can walk
I can talk
I can feel
I can hear

That's physical

But if I want the spiritual, through Christ I can hear spiritually
Talk spiritually
Feel spiritually
Hear spiritually

Truth be told if it wasn't for the connection I would not be able to say I can do all things.

If I really was to flat out say it I would say I can do nothing without God.

He says when I get to the end of my physical rope my spiritual strength kicks in.

The first half other verse displays what we can do; but the last half shares how we can do it.

Paul was in prison, explaining to them I have learned whatever happens to me to be content.

He wasn't saying he would get everything he desired, he simply says I know how to be happy with nothing as if I had everything.

Listen to the way Paul says this;

I can do all things; otherwise I will not let where I am determine who I am.

Who I am will determine where I go.

Thermometer Christians- They only register the temperature in the room. Thermostat Christians- they set the room's temperature.

I.   The Secret- verse 11

   A. Circumstances do not describe who I am.

    1. Romans 8:28- Doesn't matter what's going on, we should know.
    2. How can we know when we utter I can't?
      a. I can't make it
      b. I can' take it
      c. I can't see…
      d. I can't understand

   B. Because Paul says one thing I do know is that this will all, notice how again this word

A-l-l shows back, all of this will work together.

Now we do know that work is not an easy task.

Work requires effort, sweat, tears, and utilization of strength.

So it tells me if may not feel good but it will pan out, and the end result will be that I can.

   C. Paul hints at the outcome when he says good of them….

1. But then he slides something in that we often forget… we have to be THE CALLED…according to his purpose.
2. There is a subtle suggestion at the end that screams for attention, the only way to be THE CALLED is to be connected somehow to Him.
   a. If I was to say that is the Gray's the only way you could be a part of that is if you were to be connected somehow, presumably by marriage.

II.   The Satisfaction- verse 12

   A. Materialistic Minded people begin to be hampered by their own happiness.

   1. He says I know how to have and how not to have; and remain the same person.
   2. Otherwise some folk are only happy by what they have.
   3. Some folk feel they are somebody by what they possess.

   B. Paul politely places before us the objective of getting ourselves to not be happy with what, but be happy with whom.

   1. Psalm 1:2
      a. Delight meaning pleasure, desire.
         1. All I need is Him and the other will come.

III.   The Salutation- verse 13

   A. The connection makes the difference.

   1. He almost salutes as he speaks as if to say I did it but with you was it possible.

   B. John 15:7

   1. Otherwise if you stay where you need to be, you will not be unhappy.

2. If you stay with me, and my words stay with you, otherwise if I am in you can't would never drip from your mouth.

3. Think about it, have you ever heard Jesus say "I can't"
   No so if he has never said it and he is truly in us; how can we utter "we can't"

4. We can do whatever we desire if we are in Him.

It's about being hooked up to the right source.
That's why Paul later says: But my God...

Otherwise I've learned how to go without and to remain humble with but since I got hooked up, and stopped saying I can't...

My God shall.

Listen how introduces this nineteenth verse.

I know how to live with
I know how to live without
I know I can

But... My God shall- a promise supply all of my needs according to what he has up there!!!!!

Some people never try because so many people have told them they can't

You ought to declare tonight:
Yes I can!!!!!!!!!!!!!!

Lecture One

"The Theology In Myrmecology"
Prov. 6:6-9, Prov. 30:25

Proverbs 6:6-9 Go to the ant, thou sluggard; consider her ways, and be wise: Which having no guide, overseer, or ruler, provideth her meat in the summer, and gathereth her food in the harvest.

Solomon almost takes us on a virtual tour and teaches us the lessons on leadership that we should glean from the ant.

When Solomon speaks, he is speaking to his son but more importantly to us...

Watch how he inserts a peculiar word in the midst of this abnormal request...he says consider- consider in Hebrew means: RAHH-AHH, which is a causative term.

It means it drives to do something...you joyfully look upon...you have to respect what you behold...gain vision from.

But not only does he suggest to actually learn and apply what we see to what we do, but he then scolds us for lack thereof...the ants, which have no guide, overseer, or ruler...still provides.

As if to say they do not even have a leader at this point and make more progress than we.

Doctor M. E. Lyons

Listen to the close of the verse before we dig any deeper: and gathereth her food in the harvest…an ant has more sense than us…harvest is plenteous but the laborers are few…

Now watch the ant only has 250,000 brain cells and we have better than ten million and they will harvest what is available while we sit around and watch it dwindle away.

Introduction: Solomon here speaks of being a sluggard, one who lives with ease, attains idleness, sticks to nothing, and brings nothing to pass.

What really happens is that the person is very careless in the work before them.

Man is supposed to be the wisest creature but here the wisest man challenges us to learn from the meanest and smallest of creatures.

Watch this when we become busy; one of the components to bring about the furtherance in the kingdom is tithes and offering; if we are sluggards we become indicted in Malachi 3: 8-10.

(I won't go too far into this but even ants teach us how to tithe…they bring the meat into the house so others might benefit…)

So the first lesson the ants teach us that as Leaders we must tithe…and tithe first that others may follow…

(Commercial with father and son smoking…I am the first person to put my tithes in the plate because as Leader the folk need to see you tithe but they need to follow you tithing…)

What Solomon actually does is compare us to sleep before he ever brings up the concept of being slothful.

You know that the last few moments of sleep are always the best moments…

He literally says do not be caught taking in a few more moments of sleep whilst you neglect the work.

It does not mean we should never rest; it simply and succinctly suggests that we should never rest when we should be running…

The other prong to this is we have so many leaders now that have become lazy in their leadership, and when you become lazy in leadership it will cause a lacking in the listening.
(Because you do know the more work folk see you do the more apt they are to listen!)

The issue here is our perception of when we should work has been altered by the invasion of sleep…and sleep renders us unavailable to clearly assess what is transpiring around us.
(Eutychus…Work while it is day!) Acts 20: 7-12

The ant is used here because he/she uses its energy economically.

There are two components that make for a better leader/worker…they are prudent-careful in providing for the future, wise in practical matters and they possess forethought-thinking of something beforehand, previous consideration.
(Deal with those two…)

It is a gross presumption to be a sluggard and then expect divine provisions in the hour of need.

Now understand this: They are able to lift 20 times their own body weight. That means that if I had their strength I could lift approx. 4000 lbs. Ants have been found to build structures 500 times their own height. The life expectancy of an ant is 45-60 days. Yet these tiny creatures accomplish much in their short life-span.
Philippians 4:13- is what they live by…without even knowing!

You see the issue here is many of us want the position but we neglect the preparation that leads to progress…notice the ants prepares so that when it comes time to partake they have more than enough.

I. <u>There must be a plan</u>

Proverbs 29:18- You see the word vision in this text means to behold...look at...gaze at...to be in a trance almost...

Now understand NO LEADER can receive a VISION from anyone they hardly make eye contact with...

In order to receive a vision for where you are you must see Him where you are at!

There MUST be a plan/Vision...without the Church/Auxiliary dies...

The Living Bible says it like this: Where there is ignorance of God; the people run wild...

Now consider this...the ants are not running wild they are working in concert...one MIND; one GOAL...

A leader cannot expect greatness when there has been no investment...you see this is cause and effect...

Your following is strictly a direct reflection of your resemblance...we will come back to this point!

John Maxwell an expert on leadership in his book which we speak about certain aspects tonight says there is a law of Navigation that says: Any one can steer the ship but a true leader charts the course...

You have to know where you are going for the people to have confidence in you...that is why Paul says follow me as I follow Christ!

At first glance at an anthill, you just see a lot of activity. Ants running around everywhere.... but they have a plan.

I believe that there are a lot of believers who are active and churches that are filled with programs.... but they have no plan.

There should be a question we ask...what is the purpose of this Church... if they don't know; there is NO PLAN...

They have no vision for the future. They have little if any idea as to what their function is, and which way they are going.

As leaders most importantly a CHURCH we must have a vision, we must be as wise as ants. We must make all that we do, count for the kingdom.

Every organization, every committee, every class within the church should be geared towards reaching people, and teaching people!

II. <u>There must be participation</u>

Romans 12: 4, 5- I must hurriedly tell you that we cannot expect to lead if we are not willing to follow as well...

Take a look at an anthill and you will not see many if any ants just sitting around or standing around doing nothing.

Everyone one of those ants have a job, and no one has to tell them what it is....and no one has to push them to do it!

I wish that we could be that way as a church. Many folks would lose their job if they worked on their job the way they do for the Lord.

We often do things half-way, throw things together at the last moment.... put little if any time or planning into our efforts.

We show up for the last minute unprepared! If people ran their business the way that we operate at the house of God sometime.........the businesses would go bankrupt!

And there so busy doing what their supposed to do that they don't have time to fight among themselves!

Col. 3:17 And whatsoever ye do in word or deed; do all in the name of the Lord Jesus.

In this scripture above he says we may not all have the same office which is interpreted as function or to execute…

Now catch this: it literally means that if we are not executing our function things will not work out the way they were designed to work out…

This is about to bless you; you know how it is that ants can do so much in such a little time…everybody is functioning TOGETHER…let me come closer…you know why Hispanics and sometimes even Caucasians accomplish so much quickly…they know their function and execute…

I have a saying I have implemented in all of my Pastorates- RUN IN YOUR OWN LANE…if this is done BIG things can be done!

THE LAW OF VICTORY- this law teaches that the leader finds a way for the team to win…

It's not about you…its first about God and then about the TEAM…

TEAMWORK makes the TEAM WORK!

III. <u>There must be peace</u>

Ephesians 4:3 Endeavoring to keep the unity of the Spirit in the bond of peace.

One of the reasons that ants can get so much accomplished despite their size and in such a small amount of time is because of harmony.

Psalms 133:1 Behold how good and how pleasant it is for brethren to dwell together in unity!

This said scripture teaches us that endeavoring says to use speed; to make an effort...IT DIOES NOT SAY IT WOULD BE EASY...but there must be an effort!

The LAW OF BUY-IN- shares with us that people buy into the leader and then into the vision...

If you don't have a good relationship because of unrest or disagreements... the vision will not come to fruition!

Mending and making relationship is pivotal in making the Vision work!

IV. <u>Ants Teach Us A Lesson About Partnership.</u>

I Thessalonians 5:11

A quote from an evolutionist:
"On their own, each ant's behavior is relatively useless, but when swarms of ants come together, the patterns optimize naturally and allow them to accomplish tasks that should be far beyond their reach.

<u>There is solidarity</u>

The ant colony is a community. They build these colonies sometimes to a depth of 35 feet below the ground....it is like a city for ants.

There is complex building with rooms for various activities. They all live together in this colony.

You very seldom see an ant by itself. They live together as a family and work together as a team to get done what needs to be done.

We as believers we are co-laborers with the Lord. We have to work together, and pull together or we'll pull apart!

THE LAW OF CONNECTION- The leader touches a heart before they ask for a hand...

Show a person how much you care and then they will listen…

Maxwell partners with this scripture and teaches us that when folk know we care for them they will most likely do what it is we need them to do; but we must be careful that our mindset is team oriented and not self-oriented!

V. Ants Teach Us a Lesson about Preparedness

The scripture we are evaluating tonight speaks about being slothful… lethargic…

Ants don't know the meaning of procrastination! They don't wait till the weather turns cold before they are preparing.

They gather food while it is still warm and take it into their colony! Many of those who work hard all day will never eat of the food they are preparing because they will die before cold weather……but they want to make certain that their families are taking care of.

V7. "Provideth her meat in the summer, and gathereth her food in the harvest and gathereth her food in the harvest.

They prepare for their future.

Would you learn a lesson from these tiny creatures designed by God? They are looking to the future each day. They are preparing for what lies ahead.

The law of Legacy-A leaders lasting value is measured by succession…

First we are a terrible leader when the ministry or auxiliary we lead dies when we die!

We are to setup for those coming behind us…

Sometimes we hold onto offices and positions and never share with anyone else how do our job that our selfishness puts the team at risk!

Be it: Pastors, Evangelists, Teachers, Presidents, Chairperson(s), Directors or whatever!

Train someone…but not only train someone; leave them in better shape than you are in! Transference of Leadership…

VI. <u>The Ants Teach Us a Lesson about Perseverance</u>

Galatians 6:9- DON'T GIVE UP…it may get hard but stay in the race!

Ants have an amazing ability to survive all kinds of weather. They adapt well no matter the circumstances, and are very resilient.

You ever notice how quickly they recover when you destroy one of their colonies. They immediately start to repair the damage done. Ants aren't quitters. They persevere.

<u>Through danger</u>
Though they are so small many times we do not even notice them…. They pack a powerful punch if you mess with them.

<u>Through disaster</u>
You can run over an anthill with lawn mowers……kick it over…and they'll build it back! Ants aren't quitters!

We must not succumb to the bite of procrastination…we must press on even through this sleeping age!

<u>The ant also knows the seasons-the cycle of life.</u>

The sting of sarcasm comes through in the caricature of the sluggard.

Verse 10 in Proverbs offers an excuse, I'm not lazy at all, and I am only snatching a slight sleep, seizing the opportunity to become refreshed.

You may call it snoozing; but while your eyelids rest your poverty will panhandle everything you own…

Lecture Two

"Understanding Life"
Romans 12: 1, 2

This is text has been researched and lifted to be one of the most difficult texts in the bible due to its fullness of meaning.

<u>Two wills that are experienced by Christians.</u>

- ✓ Submissive Will-What God wants to take place
- ✓ Permissive Will- What God will allow to take place.

(1.) Presentation-Present your bodies a living sacrifice
(2.) Holy Disposition- Holy- means to be morally and spiritually excellent or perfect, and to be revered.
(3.) Acceptability disclaimer (I don't want it if) - you do know what acceptable means don't you it means worth something; it actually means something worth accepting.

On the other hand, it simply suggests that if you are going to do something for the Lord let it be something that he would want.

Don't just do it because everybody else is doing it.

Let it be something worth having.

I don't want something that you really don't want to give me, because that takes the sincerity out of giving it to me.

4. Minimum maintenance- something you keep up with; Car maintenance, if you don't keep it up it will break down on you.

You have to keep it oiled up
Tuned up
Cleaned up
Kept up
In order for it to keep starting up

Negative choice- "Do not conform any longer to the pattern of this world"

(Conform is to be a copy of an original)
When Paul so strangely suggests that we ought not to conform what he was saying indefinitely was that we ought to dictate to those who don't know the way that is right.

- Otherwise if the truth is the truth; by all means treat it and present it as the truth.
- Don't make loopholes; excuses; ways of escapes from the absolute interpretation of what it was originally intended; that is why Paul says don't conform to the world.

Because when the world needs a solution the world makes a law; the world finds a way of escape to better fit the way they wish to live.

-Abortion- passed the law to accept it.
-Divorce- easily obtainable; harder to get married than it is to become divorced
-Child rearing- CPS
-Same sex marriages- bills are being passed
Conforming to the world

When we begin interpreting the word incorrectly

When we began to mishandle this majestic mandate; we commence to pleasing the world and become displeasing to God

Look there we are almost back at the beginning again; whenever you conform to what ain't God you're not really working for God.

Watch this;
How can I present my body to somebody that I am not working for?

Present or present or present the same spelling but synonymous almost in meaning.

One word three meanings

But then again three meanings but point in the same direction.

God says I am the same yesterday, today and forever. Hebrews 13:8

Present on the order of saying if you want to know the description of what the Divine is asking for.

Present is yielding that I want somebody that is a present presenter in their presentation.

-I don't need someone who used to be a sacrifice, or will be a sacrifice; what he needs is someone to be a (right now) present living sacrifice.

Ok that's the first present, secondly is present I hope I don't lose you when you give someone a (gift) present it's usually something that they desire, follow me here

He says present your bodies as a living sacrifice; he strategically says that if you want to get me a present-gift then give me your bodies as something present-right now

That's two what about the third one there is (introduction) present; well now we know the mindset of the sacrifice that should be given; what it should be;

Then what's left is how to give it; present it; offer introduce or exhibit.

It's like this Offer the gift of being who we ought to be introducing. BE NOT CONFORMED.

- ❖ We ought to take no part in them being the frontrunners (We have to allow certain things to go unnoticed in order to reach the new age. We need to be Non-denominational in order to say I am not associating with any denominations.)
- ❖ We ought to be that light that shineth in darkness
- ❖ We are to be trendsetter and not the world

(2.) Positive Call- "Be transformed by the renewing of your mind"

If we spend enough time with Him, you will start thinking differently

A. What it Proves

(4.) The proof is in the pudding- the writer says the believer must prove the will of God.

Prove means to both find and follow…prove here is used in applying to metals, trying them to the severity of fire; to explore, to ascertain.

(Wilson Chambers; explain-obey)

- • The only way to find and follow God's will is to keep your mind upon the things of God. (That good means to investigate; because everything that glitters ain't gold, and everything that shines bright, grass greener)

The word good here is an adjective (modify or describe a noun) agreeing with the noun will.

Otherwise His will is good; or we can find His Will by finding what is that good.

a. Perfect- (teleios) without error or mistake, flawless, complete, absolute, free from any need, short of nothing, completely fulfilled.

It points back at the introduction and says when you have become perfect you will; Present your bodies.

Paul had to use these adjectives appositionally, as a word describing the next move; placing a word there to better describe, to convey to us the severity, and sincerity of this text.

("Do not be conformed") is from the Greek term schēma, which implies an "external semblance."

Let your outside look like your inside...Out of the heart flow the issues of life...the heart reports to the mind

If the heart reports to the mind, the mind reports to the face to display what is on the inside; how can we have the outside resemble the inside?

Get our minds right; when there is pain on the inside it shows up on the outside by way of our face.

Then he says THIS is the will of God!!!

Lecture Three

"Modeling His Methods Through Equipping"
Matthew 4: 18-20

I was almost thrown as to whether or not to use the thematic scripture or another obvious scripture.

The theme in Ephesians speaks of the mission concerning the method.

But this particular scripture deals with the method through a certain vehicle and it speaks in specificity of how to get the job done.

Method means procedure; modus operandi.

Equipping means to furnish; the word MAKE suggests that he will take whatever material that is available and cause it to benefit the awaiting catch.

Make pay-eh-oh to form or author.
To form references Genesis to take what is and cause it to be.

He took what he had and made it work!

But when you speak about author it suggests that your end production is taken from existing information.

Just like Preachers we begin to lay claim and possession on Preachments; but the truth is we are just authoring homilies that are compiled of existing materials.

No person is original in their information only in their presentation.

The only fresh is the vantage point from which we take.

He could have chosen eminent scribes and Pharisees to publish the Gospel; but he chose unlearned fishermen.

No credit or authority.

He chose the inadequate.
Men made ministers run ruin the heritage of God.

When the scripture mentions Jesus it does not mention his name as belonging to the text but for the sake of a lesson.

Peter and John were already disciples this was a call to SERVICE. John 1:35.

He called them from just standing to serving.

You are standing when there is motion but no mission.

You are standing when you are acting but not affecting.

1st principle: there must be true examination- He saw them; deal with the word saw.

Notice how the scene begins; it commences by saying Jesus walking and He SAW!

He was not aimlessly wayfaring He was observant in His travels.

I know it is juvenile; but in order to see one has to be looking!

Our problem is seldom do we look.

We are so caught up in us we have no time to observe others.
We are inundated with our own egocentric expeditions that we pay no mind to positive prospects.

Secondly, might I say; looking does not happen in the synagogue; it happens outside the temple walls.

Carefully consider the text before us; it says Jesus was walking by the sea!

If I could speak boldly; He went where the fish were biting.

Our hang up is that we position ourselves in this inviting yet comatose state of looking in house when the search should be taking place outside the house!

He saw them not they saw Him!

2nd principle: There should be an invitation.

He says to Peter and Andrew: Follow me.

In order to be a true invitation; you must have a real destination.
I cannot follow you somewhere you are not sure of going yourself.

Invitation without a destination ends up causing deterioration.

Think about it; when a person spends their lives merely existing it allows retrogression to take place.

Let me say it another way; without a vision the people perish.

In other words, you can invite folk; but if the folk you have invited are not taken to a prosperous place; their fate is to perish!

That's why so many Churches suffer now; they are big on invitation but so feeble on destination.

They have a house full; but have no real word to carry them to a certain place.

They have programs; but no purpose.

They have revivals but no regeneration.

There are musicals but have no message.

There are districts but no direction.

There are conventions but no contractions.

I know you probably missed the last one.

Anything that is of God should at some point and time cause contractions; new life!

3rd <u>principle:</u> You must share your expectation.

The truth is our expectation must be God's expectation.

He simply says the direct object is: fishers of men!

You are to be focused on men (women).

Our goal should be to reach men.

Not finances
Not a full house
Not mega status
Not to be a Bishop

But to reach men.

We have misconstrued our purpose of coming together.

Yes, we should meander on the outside of the Church but when we come together our expectations should align themselves with God's expectation.

His altruistic goal is to cause us to be fishers of men.

I am aware of the fact that many times we because of our statuses we tend to mistake His expectation with our expectation.

Consider this: on eve level possible; we are so much lifting our expectation over His; we come together and call out names.

Doctor so in so gave so much and so on.
Why are we coming together; is it for the sake of men or is it for the sake of money?

4th <u>principle:</u> there was abdication (give up) from their current situation.

Look there in the text; it says that straightway left their nets.

They forsook their priority to possess His priority.
<u>(Just as Dean Walls alluded to on last evening; Martha had dispositioned her mission)</u>

Watch this: they did not put their nets up.

They did not ask for him to cast their nets one more time.

They did not question his invitation.

They did not try and rewire His expectation.

They simply dropped what they were doing and followed Jesus.

They LEFT their nets.

Immediate obedience.

Their nets were their means for living.

Their leaving the nets were like leaving their full property and displaying their interest.

They forsook all for the sake of Jesus.

They left the known for the unknown.

They were pursuing the sure in pursuit of the unsure.

Leave notoriety for the forgotten.

Walk away from the certainty of a livelihood for the uncomfortable life of servant hood.
Jesus took what they were doing and gave them an invisible promotion.

They were fishers of food; and he says to them I will make you fishers of men.
God usually calls those who are busy doing something!

They were cast-<u>ING</u> in action.

Saul was searching for his daddy's donkeys
David was keeping his daddy's sheep
The shepherds were guarding their flocks
Amos was farming in Tekoa
Matthew was at a tax collectors table
Moses was seeing after his daddy in laws sheep
Gideon was threshing wheat.

Following Jesus costs!

It means leaving something's behind.

Woman left her pitcher
Matthew left his table

Bartimaeus left his cloak
Legion left his craziness
(Clothed in his right mind)

So it is simple when it comes to modeling His methods through equipping we are SHOW; KNOW; GO!

Question does this mean always meeting up here or meeting out there?

If I had to sum this thought up in one statement concerning the text it would simply be:

The disciple is to go where the fish are swimming!

Relevant Biblical Preaching
March 17th @ 2:30pm- 10-minute synopsis

- It is one's life that renders relevancy rather than what they relay!
- Relevancy is better received when our lives match our lips! Luke 22:32
- Preaching must be received in our places of dwelling before it can ever be received in our places of Worship.
- Our behavior should hold hands with our beliefs.
- We cannot share that which we do not eat! Ezekiel had to eat the scroll.
- Haddon Robinson says: A relevant and biblical sermon should be a bullet and not a buckshot- a buckshot is all over the place and has no intended goal in mind! A bullet is directed at a specific target and if aimed correctly it will hit the mark!

1. I read a quote the other day that said, "Old fashioned preaching is not relevant to the needs of modern man." How can our preaching be both biblically relevant and modern while maintaining validity to the teachings of scripture?

Firstly, old fashioned preaching is as alive today as it was in the days of old. His word does not change, however the particular needs have swayed!

Doctor M. E. Lyons

We can retain validity and relevancy in our biblical preaching by correctly exegeting scripture to meet the present need of the congregation we are charged to feed!

Next, we cannot be relevant in our biblical preaching if we are not staying on the wall as scripture has prescribed. Isaiah 62:6

2. In his book on preaching, entitled "Between Two Worlds", Derek Morris talks about listening, to God and to the Word of God, but listening to the voices of the modern world as well. What are your thoughts on that and how does or should it influence preaching?

Rienhold Niebuhr and Karl Barth is said to have stated that a preacher must preach with a bible in one hand and a newspaper in the other in order to maintain relevancy in our proclamation.

This does not influence our preaching it makes our preaching applicable to the man/woman who is in our midst.

3. When it comes to preaching how can we strike a balance between biblical integrity and cultural relevancy.

Do as Paul ascribed and that is be all to all. I Corinthians 9:22

Cultural boundaries can be erased if we made the effort to BECOME! This word became in Greek shares the connotation of behavior or

GEN-erate and GEN means that which produces!

In the book The Big Idea Of Biblical Preaching Wilhite and Gibson says: we reach every culture when we share our human experiences and allow our transparency to dispel the age old mindset of we are better than the rest.

General Questions:

1. What is the role of the Pastor in the church, culture, and community?

The role of the Pastor is quite simple and should be universal concerning church, culture, and community; SHOW, SEARCH, and SHARE. To show LIGHT, to search for the LOST, and to share the LORD!

2. Should a Pastor be prophetic? Should the Pastor simply maintain the status quo?

Absolutely, a Pastor should be prophetic in the message God has uploaded to him! (It has been stated that the Word is not downloaded from Heaven through our head, but rather only given when we apply our posterior to a seat and study) If we are in constant communication with God what we share is what we were sent!

A Pastor should not continue with the status quo. Scripture says that we are a peculiar people and if we are to be leaders of other peculiar people it becomes a conflict of interest to maintain the status quo.

3. Millennials (born in the 80's or 90's- Generation Y) are leaving the church in droves and one of the reason that is given is that they say the church has no goals, they do the same things every week, its predictable and much of what we do has nothing to do with bible as much as it is our tradition, "this is how we have always done it."

The church has not been guilty of setting goals. We cannot be so antiquated and narrow minded that we are lackadaisical in goal setting that we simply use the escape goat of we use the Bible alone. Using this route is like saying I have to go to California by way of driving with the keys in our hands and never have the goal of placing the key in the ignition.

Goals are the tools that allow the parishioners to catch a glimpse of the vision that we have so clearly seen!

4. One of the growing challenges in this postmodern time is that church views culture as the enemy. My question is how can we reach people who we never engage? And the next question is, whether it's our responsibility to change them or introduce them to the change agent?

We will never reach those we fear and have not faced. We are to introduce them to that which can change them. It is never ours to grow the seed only to plant it! The seed changes simply by the process of nature!

5. Community is not something that is passive with millennials; it is essential, and I'm not talking about fake and phony but real and authentic community. How do we create community in the church and engage community outside the church?

Remove traditionalism and ritualistic acts that have no salvific implications. Millennials are more interested in not what will keep me out of Heaven, but what will get me in Heaven.

In other words, this generation we now speak of is concerned about free worship! There is nothing wrong with this, because Jesus ascribes the very same thing, he that worships me must worship me in spirit and in truth!

We create community outside the church by implementing core and community groups to meet in other places outside of church such as: book clubs, study groups, and focused ministry groups: singles, couples, young adults, widows and widowers etc.

Mark 3:31-34

Commentaries

Coach Earley-Don't be so quick to judge another man's actions before you learned the reason for his action. Everyone has a story; so listen more than you talk: the story may contain the key to your blessing. Take time to listen to all of God's people that are in your life; their wisdom is priceless.

About the Author

Doctor M. E. Lyons has felt the calling of God on his life from his youth and was called into the gospel ministry in 1980 at the tender age of four. Doctor M. E. Lyons is married to the beautiful Latish Luckey-Lyons, and they have four wonderful children: Deja Lyons, Myron E. Lyons II, Jeremiah M. E. Lyons, and Benjamin M. E. Lyons.

He has authored nine books entitled: Fresh Air Volume One, The Mind: The Pulpit of God, The Testimony of the Sheep: According to Psalms 23 (a weekly devotional guide), 52 Weeks of Grace: Edition One, Sermons and Illustrations by M. E. First Series, Fresh Air Volume Two, Lessons and Lectures to Live By, A Guide to Grieving, and Smile . . . It Becomes You. Currently, there are seven other books in the process of being published, ranging from second volumes and books concerning marriage/ relationships, an autobiography, and a novel on the contrasts of men and women. He has written several songs, poems, and stage plays, and he has also starred in the hit stage play STAT with national recording artist Don Diego. There's a CD (single) featuring Doctor Lyons that has been recently released.

He has attended D. Edwin Johnson Baptist Institute (a seminary) in pastoral studies, evangelism, New Testament survey, Old Testament survey, southern Baptist heritage, and the late Doctor Hardin L. Ward was the instructor. He has attended Dallas Institute of Funeral Services in pursuit of an associate degree in applied sciences in 2005. He underwent music theory with Bernice Abrams-Dallas, Texas. He has also obtained a bachelor of science degree in psychology in applied behavioral analysis, Kaplan University, Davenport, Iowa. He has obtained a master of arts degree in theological studies with emphasis on apologetics and philosophy in Lynchburg, Virginia, from Liberty University. He has obtained a master of arts degree in religious education from Liberty University in Lynchburg, Virginia. He has also received a master of divinity in theology from Liberty University. He has also received a doctorate in divinity from Saint Thomas Christian University in Jacksonville, Florida.

In 2011 he received the necessary invitation from Dr. Joel Gregory to attend Oxford University in London, England, and received certification in homiletics and hermeneutics, and he obtained the necessary requirements to become a distinguished gentleman of Oxford. While there, he preached at the Cote Church in the UK.